Europe Through My Eyes

Travel Memoir

ISBN: 978-93-7424-047-2
Price: ₹240.00
Publishing Year 2025

Published by:
Crown Publishing
Head Office: 3rd Floor, Binue, Bilaspur,
Chhattisgarh 495006
Phones: +91 77228 14335
Email: publish@crownpublishing.in
Website: www.crownpublishing.in

Europe Through My Eyes

Travel Memoir

Mahendra Pratap

CROWN
PUBLISHING

Translator's Note

This English edition of the memoir *"Europe Through My Eyes"* is a faithful translation of the original Hindi work *"Meri Europe Yatra"*, authored by Mahendra Pratap.

The translation has been carefully undertaken by **Rashmi Singh**, who holds an MBA in Agribusiness (Gold Medalist) and a B.Sc. in Agriculture (Gold Medalist). With deep respect for the author's experiences and insights, every effort has been made to retain the spirit, emotion and authenticity of the original narrative, making it accessible to a wider audience.

Translator's Address:
8590 Magnolia Trail,
Eden Prairie, Minnesota, USA
Zip Code – 55344

Table of Content

*****

Blessings

"Europe Through My Eyes" is the first work of Mahendra Pratap, a senior advocate of Patna High Court, to be published in the form of a book. I believe that readers will certainly be impressed by his writing talent. The reason is that even before this, his writings have been published in magazines and newspapers and compiled in books. His first work was published during the JP movement, which was related to his jail visit. I am extremely happy within the publication of this book because I was the only one who got the opportunity to publish the said touching memoir.

Actually, there is a coordination of various talents in his personality. After taking MBA and law degrees, he first adopted the profession of semi-government service. But, his self-respecting nature, independent temperament and desire to do something in the future did not allow him to stay in the limited sphere there for long. As a result, he returned to his favorite field of politics and social service. In a short time, he also got success in both these fields. In the field of politics, he achieved a high position at the provincial level and good popularity among the people through social service. Apart from the profession of a lawyer, he was also successful in the field of industry and business due to his MBA degree. Apart from all this, as an efficient and successful parent, he provided higher education to his two sons and his only daughter. Today, his family is equally blessed by both goddesses Lakshmi and Saraswati. With apologies to the readers, I would like to say that I have such an intimate relationship with the author that he not only gives me the respect of an elder brother, but like a younger brother, he is always ready to serve me in every way according to his nature, due to which I could not resist the temptation of discussing a little about this inspiring personality.

Now, as far as this book is concerned, it may seem small in terms of the number of pages, but by packing the ocean in a pot, the author has made it a storehouse of knowledge. In short, the readers easily get acquainted with the past and present, history and geography, civilization and culture, religion and rituals, conduct and thoughts, customs and traditions, lifestyle, faith and tradition, food and drink, industry and trade etc. of the European countries described in this book. The usefulness of the book has increased further with the description of natural beauty, state of education, various products, architecture and paintings, historical monuments etc. Apart from these, this book can also act as a guide for those going there by mentioning traffic rules, government system, facilities of trains and other water and land vehicles, hotels and restaurants, the process of going to those countries and the necessary documents etc.

The book uses compound style everywhere, avoiding verbosity of language. The choice of words is so accurate that every line will give you some information. The reader does not get bored anywhere, rather he remains delighted by happily diving into this ocean filled in a pitcher and picking pearls. The language is simple and understandable, and the style is understandable. Every place mentioned has come alive. There is spontaneity, simplicity and interest in the expression of all the subjects described. It seems that the author has not only seen the scenes there with his eyes but has also captured them with the movie camera of his heart, which keeps appearing before the readers like a movie. This makes it seem that the readers are not reading the book but are travelling to that place themselves. All this has given the book such an amazing ability to keep the readers hooked that there is no peace without finishing it in one sitting.

In the end, I welcome such a successful work on travel literature and congratulate the author for this and wish him a bright future in the field of writing.

Ravindra Kumar
+91-9431807721
Senior journalist and writer, Patna

Preface

Writer Mahendra Pratap, who is a mature social activist with intellectual capacity and is also an advocate in the Patna High Court, appears in his book "Europe Through My Eyes" with a holistic and comprehensive vision. Firstly, the mature experience of social and political life and the court's approach to see and understand any object, any scene, is blessed in every step of his journey and in the words of this book.

Recently, he along with his wife Nirmala, son Shiv Pratap and daughter-in-law Priyanka visited many countries of Europe and their important cities and shared what they saw and understood on social media. During the journey, wherever he went in Europe, after seeing the realities of social, economic, political, business and cultural life very closely, he prepared an article at every stop and posted it on his Facebook. This book is a collection of all those articles which should be accepted as a heritage of the intellectual society.

His visit was not just for fun, it was an intellectual effort to know Europe in its entirety, in which he has proved to be completely successful. During the last four decades, I have had the opportunity to read the travel memoirs of great personalities, thinkers, archaeologists, politicians, cultural activists, habitual tourists, etc. Many of the memoirs were very good, some new information was also received, but there is no hesitation in saying that most of them were onesided or a reflection of the writer's ideological commitment. Some looked at countries through the prism of politics, others through the prism of reaffirming their ideological commitments. Some were limited to just having fun, while some were immersed in the unfathomable beauty of nature. The writers also prepared their memoirs by looking at the history and culture there from a one-sided perspective.

This journey of Mahendra Pratap took place with full openness. Everywhere he stands with a liberal and broad outlook. That is why this book touches both the hearts and minds of the readers, telling the story of the harmony of nature and development, past and present, tradition and science, faith and non-faith, trade and practice, and religion and culture.

The Czech Republic, Italy, Austria, Germany and Switzerland are home to many historically famous cities of Europe, their cultural and tourist places, lakes, waterfalls, beautiful valleys of mountains, monuments, museums, In addition to presenting word pictures of different shades of folk and urban life. The author studied the forms of government of these countries in totality.

His depth of study can be considered as the greatest feature of this book. The special thing is that during his journey, writer Mahendra Pratap tried to reach the historical places and characters with which Shakespeare had given immortal works to world literature.

The city of Venice in Italy is the sixth stop of the author's journey, where he is reminded of Shakespeare's book "The Merchant of Venice". Obviously , the author must have read this book in his student days, so his memory trace remained in this journey as well. There can be no dynamic and serious reader of English language and literature without reading Shakespeare.

The city is a thriving business hub. It is settled on small sea islands, it is also called the floating city. Taking a lesson from the information provided by the author about the modern development of rail transport management here, the Indian

Railways should also be equipped with state-of-theart technology and set the destination of development. The maximum speed of the train in Italy is 260 kilometers per hour. There is a major tourist destination called Verona, 115 kilometers from Venice. Shakespeare's world-famous play "Romeo and Juliet" is centered on the lovers of this place. Juliet's house attracts literary tourists from all over the world. The building dates back to the fourteenth century in the same balcony Juliet waited for Romeo. These two names, go to any corner of the world, people associated with literary style are just like the names of Laila-Majnu and Heer-Ranjha in the Indian subcontinent. Another Shakespearean play centered on Verona is "The Two Gentlemen of Verona".

Indian festivals in the Czech Republic are celebrated with as much reverence and enthusiasm as in India. This is described very vividly by the author. This indicates that irrespective of the country, all are bound by the thread of cultural unity, despite being different in form. It is an exemplary characteristic of the people of Indian origin that wherever they reside, they do not allow their culture to be separated from theirs. Holi is celebrated in June every year in Prague, the capital of the Czech Republic, and the panoramic Rath Yatra of Lord Jagannath is taken out by the local unit of ISKCON. The specialty is that along with the people of Indian origin, many Europeans also participate in the festival and present an unforgettable view of brotherhood.

In conclusion, it can be said that this book is an intellectual gift from the author in the repository of travel literature. The language style of the book and the way of presenting the facts are simple, easy which adds to its usefulness. The book is readable and collectible. It is a speaking document of the politics, governance, living conditions, behavior of the people, industrial progress, technological development, management of transport, art-culture, tourism, their relations with India etc.

For those who have never been to Europe or who are unlikely to go in the future, this is like an experienced and skilled guide. Thank you to the author for making the intellectual society and the new generation aware of his travel memoirs.

Surendra Manpuri
Journalist,
Former Bureau Chief , Chhapra and Hajipur Unit,
Hindustan Hindi Daily.
9835635480

My Perspective

The idea of traveling to Europe had never crossed my mind. I had not even imagined the publication of a book on travel memoirs, but the positive competitive thinking of the children made the trip to Europe possible, while the advice, encouragement and support of kind friends and well-wishers paved the way for the publication of the present book.

Both my sons are employed abroad for a living. The elder son has been in the Arab country "Oman" for a decade and the younger son in the Czech Republic of Europe since 2022. At the insistence and arrangement of the eldest son Shankar, the Arab country "Oman", located in the south-west of Asia, I had gone many times. Despite the strong desire and insistence of the younger son Shiv Pratap, I could not plan a trip to Europe till 2024 due to personal reasons, but I committed for 2025. In February itself, Shiv Pratap booked online appointment for the Schengen visa after depositing the Visa fee. I appeared at VFS office on the scheduled appointment with all the necessary documents and application. VFS representative verified the same and send my application to Czech republic Embassy in Delhi for approval. I received my Visa via post within 2 weeks. Indian or non-EU nationals travel to Europe only on a Schengen visa. With Schengen Visa travel is allowed in 29 European countries of the Schengen group. Single-entry visa allows one-time entry into the Schengen area, while multiple-entry visa allows freedom to travel multiple times. The visa is approved in about 15 days after the submission of the application for a Schengen visa with a valid passport, itinerary, proof of residence, financial statements, travel insurance, application fee, biometric data (fingerprint and photo) at the consulate. The application is also submitted online. France, Germany, Italy, Spain, Switzerland, Austria,

Czech Republic, etc. (total 29) countries are included in the Schengen area. There are 44 Countries in Europe and 27 member countries in the European Union.

The best time to travel to Europe for Indians is from May to August. At this time the temperature there is between 15 to 33 degrees. Otherwise, with the arrival of cold, the temperature drops to minus 20 degrees. Between December and February, the land/earth, houses, trees, etc. are covered with snow and look like cotton swabs. That's why, I planned my trip in May and June,to avoid the outbreak of cold in Europe.

Heating systems are installed in homes, offices, trains, metros, trams, buses, etc. The heating system here is mainly of two types: central and distributed. In a central heating system, heat is generated in a single location and then distributed through pipes or radiators, whereas in distributed heating systems, different heaters are mounted in each room.

It was an important moment in my life, not just travelling, but also to experience closely the governance system, lifestyle, religious, cultural conditions etc. of different countries of the world, Czech Republic, Italy, Austria, Germany, Switzerland etc.

Europe has the largest number of Christians, including Roman Catholics, Protestants, and Eastern Orthodox denominations. In Western and Central Europe, such as France, Italy, Spain, Ireland and Poland, the Roman Catholic Church is dominated, while in Eastern and Southern Europe, such as Russia, Greece, Serbia, Romania and Bulgaria, the Eastern Orthodox Church is dominated.

It is worth mentioning here that Russia is the world's largest transcontinental country spread over Eastern Europe and Northern Asia. Protestants predominate in countries like

Germany, United Kingdom, Sweden and Denmark. By the way, Christianity is based on the teachings of Jesus Christ.

Scholars have considered Christianity to be a monotheistic religion at the center of faith and tradition and have rejected polytheism and atheism. All the commandments mentioned in the Bible are at the heart of Christianity. Christianity was founded in the first century. Faith and tradition in Christianity are centered on the personality of Jesus Christ. The Holy Spirit is considered to be an aspect of God. Salvation is an important concept in Christianity, which provides salvation from sins and eternal life with God. The church has an important place in the conduct of religious activities. There is no trace of religious fanaticism among Christians in European countries. Warm-heartedness and cooperative behavior are in their daily routine. The joint family system is slowly coming to an end here. Criminal incidents like robbery, theft, pickpocketing, snatching etc. are negligible here.

Non-Christians also have a presence in Europe. Bosnia, Herzegovina, Albania, Kosovo, North Macedonia and some Russian regions have significant Muslim populations with ethnic links to Islam. Islam is also a monotheistic religion based on the Quran. Jewish communities in Europe have existed since ancient times, but this number was significantly reduced due to the Jewish genocide (Holocaust) during World War II. Followers of Buddhism, Hinduism and Sikhism also live in Europe, but their number is less.

The number of non-religious people in Europe has increased day by day. Non-religious means a class which has not associated itself with the beliefs and traditions of any established religion. The number of such classes is constantly increasing. Therefore, it can be said that in Europe Secularism and scientific progress have reduced the influence of religion, but this principle does not apply to Muslims.

Here the traffic system and traffic signaling of the cities are of high quality. Traffic police are not seen at any traffic post, yet the traffic remains quite smooth and controlled. There is a separate signal lamp at the zebra crossing for pedestrians to cross the road. Passengers cross the road only when the light of the lamp is green, but in the zebra crossing where the signal lamp is not installed, the passengers cross the road without hesitation and it is the responsibility of the driver to reconcile. Adherence to traffic rules and laws is in the behavior of the people here. In almost all major cities, buses, metros and trams or bus and tram services are operated under public transport. The entire traffic system of the city is computerized, so that the passenger gets information about the transport schedule and stoppages on mobile. The option to buy travel tickets of public transport is also available on mobile. All the stops are equipped with a computerized display board displaying the arrival and departure information of vehicles. Apart from this, online booking services of many private agencies are also available for taxis.

During my stay in Italy, I got to know and understand the train service during my visit to Florence, Pisa, Venice and Verona. All the main stations here are connected to the market complex. There is an underpass to change the platform. There is no overbridge anywhere. Information regarding arrival-departure and platform of trains is constantly displayed on the display board. Each coach has a computerized display board inside and outside. On the display board inside the bogey, the temperature (inside and outside) of the coach, the speed of the train, the information of the next station as well as the picture of the passengers sitting in the bogie is displayed, while the display board outside the bogie displays the train number and its route. All bogies are air-conditioned, since the coaches are interconnectedness , one can go to any bogie within the train. In terms of fare and convenience, the coaches of the train are divided into three categories: Standard, Premium and Business. The maximum running speed of regional trains is 160 kilometers per hour and the maximum speed of express trains is 260 kilometers per hour. Train service to Germany is even more advanced than here. In Germany, the operation of the train has started on an experimental basis with hydrogen gas. Everywhere in Europe, train, metro, tram and bus doors are automatic, which opens and closes automatically when they stop and open.

We opted for road journey to Germany, Austria and Switzerland. To protect the population from noise pollution, the glass freeway was installed as sound barrier at the place on the highway as needed. There's a Waze app for navigation across Europe, which makes road travel smooth and easy. Direction guidance to the destination, speed set for transportation on the highway, speed of the vehicle, lane information, information about any vehicle standing ahead on the road and information related to construction work comes with an alert on the screen through this app. The alarm automatically indicates when the speed of the vehicle increases beyond the prescribed limit. Everywhere the maximum speed is set for transportation on the highway. Only in Germany there is no maximum speed limit on the highway and the highway here is toll free. Air travel to Europe is also organized and accessible. Passengers are allowed to go to the boarding pass counter along with their family members.

In case of a flight delay of more than three hours, except for natural disasters and special circumstances within Europe, there is provision for the airline company to pay 600 euros

(60,000 rupees) as compensation to the passenger. Probably, this is one of the reasons for the on-time flight operations.

During the period of slavery, a conspiracy was hatched to misrepresent India's rich history and way of life in order to fuel anti-India perception on foreign soil with the help of the British rule. The British had to prove on the world stage that before the British rule, Indians were uncivilized and incompetent. At the end of the 19th century, Kunch, a professor at a university in Germany, came to India for a summer visit for three months on the reward of the British government. Mr. Kunch spent his entire time in a hotel in Shimla. Apart from the hotel, he did not go anywhere in India, but wrote many thick books on India's culture, history, art skills, social life, all of which are misleading and different from the truth. Kunch was counted not only in the university, but also in the German scholarly circle. It is discussed on pages 211-218 of Dr. Satyanarayan's book "Aware Ki Europe Yatra", published in 1938 AD by the Book Store, Laheriasarai(Bihar, India). In the preindependence era, Dr. Satyanarayana received his doctorate from University of Germany. He was fluent in several

European languages, including German, and won the Chhapra East Lok Sabha seat in independent India.

There has been a lot of change in global thinking after independence. Geographical distances have decreased. The world has become aware of the truth and reality. People's interest in India's oldest civilization and culture has increased. People of the world are feeling fortunate to come closer to the Sanatani tradition committed to the happiness and welfare of humanity (Sarvajan Sukhaya – Sarvajan Hitay) by considering the entire earth as a family (Basudhaiva Kutumbakam) for mental peace and stability. The dedication of thousands of foreign tourists in the Sanatani festivals of Holi and Jagannath Rath Yatra held in

European soil "Prague" is a direct example of this. Today, millions of Indian youth are hoisting the flag of their hard work and talent on the global horizon under the guise of their cultural traditions as the Sanatani flag bearers.

On May 9, 2025, I along with my wife Smt. Nirmala Singh had reached Delhi at 1 pm for a trip to Europe. After the Pahalgam terror incident, Pakistani terrorist bases were demolished by India on the night of 6-7th May. Pakistan's retaliatory initiative was also covered in the Pakistani border and the Pakistani military airport and strategic locations were severely damaged by the Indian Army. The situation inside the country was tense. Flights were canceled from many border airports and more flights were expected to be canceled. It was becoming difficult to pass the time in a state of doubt. There was a flight from Terminal-3 at 6 am to Istanbul, the next day. It is said that an empty mind is the devil's abode. The skepticism of the journey had disturbed my mind. It was difficult for me to pass the time. My mind was confused by all sorts of thoughts coming and going. I finally stabilized myself. In order to remove the emptiness of the mind, I started preparing the outline of the foreign trip done earlier and the possible trip. After the travel report was prepared, I posted it on my Facebook account on 10th May 2025. I had no plans to prepare a travel account and post it on Facebook regularly, but the quick comments by friends and well-wishers on the posts became a source of encouragement and strength accumulation for me. Greetings and good wishes were received through comments, but most of the friends and well-wishers were of the opinion that it was important to share the travel experience. Among them are Surendra Manpuri, author of many books and journalist former editor of Prabhat Khabar, Swayam Prakash, journalist Padmasambhava Shrivastava, Bhai Raghupati, a comrade of the seventy-four movement, Jitendra Kumar Singh, a resident of Namidih in Lalganj block and the author of many books. Ex Government Official Ram Bihari Singh, Nandlal Singh, Amrendra Kumar, Yashovardhan Rathore, General Secretary of Veer Kunwar Singh Sansthan, Pashupatinath Singh Ajay, Dr. Prakash Chandra Mishra, Social Worker Sudhir Kumar Singh of Sonepur, Manvendra Singh, Amar Tiwari, Sarangdhar Prasad Singh, Advocate Naval Singh, Awadhesh Singh of Shikarpur, Ex AGM of SBI Chandrakant Jha Pathik. I am especially grateful to Dr. Abhaynath Singh of Lalganj,Awadh Sharma, Girish Nandan Singh of Dighwara, whose comments enabled me to share the travel memoir on Facebook.

Now it was time to publish the travel memoir. I am deeply grateful to journalist Surendra Manpuri and writer and editor Jitendra Kumar Singh, a resident of Namidih, Lalganj, without their guidance and active support the publication of this book in this particular form would not have been possible.

It is necessary to quote some heartwarming comments from friends and well-wishers on Facebook, which led to a positive influx of mental strength and paved the way for the publication of the book.

Surendra Manpuri: Everything related to Europe travel that you are putting on Facebook is quite important and inspiring. I have never been to Europe but through you I am getting acquainted with all the features there. If the full account of the journey to Europe is published in the form of a book, then the intellectual society will consider it a great achievement. When you return from the trip, there will be special things on this.

Padmasambhava Shrivastava:- It is appropriate to present the entire article series in the form of a book. Publication of beautiful photographs along with the cover page and related article will prove to be effective readability of the book.

Sudhir Kumar Singh: It is a request that after returning to India from the tour, all the travelogues should be compiled by you through a book.

Nand Lal Singh: Yes, I was also going to say that if these articles of mine are collected and made memorable in the form of a book, then it will be readable and useful for everyone. Your articles are so lucid and comprehensible that reading does not fill the mind. At the last full stop, the thirst becomes even more intense.

Surendra Manpuri: I have read travelogues of many writers, but what you are writing will prove to be a golden chapter in travel literature. I have also decided on the name of the book... “My trip to Europe”.

Parent and elder brother Hindustan's former Chief Deputy Editor Ravindra Kumar said on mobile on June 1, 2025 that I have seen the post related to travel experience. It should be published in book form. Travel material and photographs will be taken.It was also an order for me. I am deeply grateful to all of them. It would be ungrateful to me not to show my gratitude to them.

Son Shiv Pratap and daughter-in-law Priyanka were responsible for arranging the entire Europe tour , but the role of supervising was the eldest son Shankar Pratap, daughterin-law Sarika, son-in-law Bhuvanesh and daughter Rashmi. All of them discharged their responsibilities honestly. As a result, they all deserve my blessings. Many of my friends have also blessed him, which I quote in the same way.

Nand Lal Singh: The devotion to duty of son Shiv Pratap and daughter-in-law Priyanka proves that Shravan Kumar and Sita are born in every era.

Sudhir Kumar Singh: Many blessings to the son and daughter-in-law. Lucky parents and God's grace. The result of the proper values given by you is that your children are devoted to you with a reverent spirit even after the foreign environment, its culture, its youthful thinking. This is the identity of the eternal.

Awadhesh Kumar Singh: I wish your son all the best and best wishes too. They are chanting Jai Shri Ram alone.

Mahendra Pratap

Europe Tour: Background

For the very first time I got the opportunity to travel Europe and the credit goes to my younger son for this opportunity. In this visit, in addition to the cultural heritage, there was an opportunity to experience the economic, social and political conditions closely. There is also a thought to be aware of the problems of youth who have arrived from India in search of employment. On 10th May 2025, I am starting the journey from Terminal 3 of Delhi International airport. It is expected to reach Prague, the capital of the Czech Republic, by 7 pm.

By the way, before this, in the name of foreign travel, I have got a chance to visit the Arab country "Oman" which is located in South-Western Asia many times. The language there is Omani Arabic. The decency and tactfulness of the people of Oman is a sign of Islamic humanity, not Islamic jihad. This was experienced automatically during cruises outside the township or encountering the natives during a walk along the beach. He raised his hands respectfully and chanted the Walekum Salam with a smile, which was followed by a spontaneous response of the raising of the hand with a smile. The people of different countries and the difference in language, yet the feeling of compassion towards each other is a symbol of humanity in the form of cultural heritage.

Oman has a monarchical form of government, which is ruled by the Sultan. The impact of good governance is clearly visible on the ground. The police administration is not visible on the streets, but there is no sign of theft, snatching and criminal incidents. This can only be gauged from the fact that in the township where my elder son lives, almost all the neighbours go to the market without locking the main gate of their houses.

At Oman's capital Muscat Airport, passengers and their family members are allowed to proceed to the boarding area. India and Oman enjoy robust bilateral trade and investment ties. Oman is classified as a high-income economy by the World Bank.

In this visit, I will try to get a comparative insight into the cultural heritage of Europe, Arab and India and its impact on its citizens. Thank you all from the bottom of my heart for God's infinite grace and the good wishes from all my friends for a successful journey. During the journey, I will try to keep you informed about every step through social media.

Beautiful view of Waldstein garden,Prague

Europe Tour - 1 (Czech Republic)

Prague, the beautiful city of stunning Architecture

As per the pre-scheduled program, on May 10th, 2025, at 8 pm, we reached Prague, the capital of the Czech Republic the European Country.

I was accompanied by my wife Nirmala Singh, Ravi Agarwal of Jamshedpur, Nikita Rungta of Cuttack, Amarjit Singh Vaidya of Pipariya (MP), Pratipal Vaidya and Renu Vaidya of Gurugram. My younger son Shiv Pratap and daughter-in-law Priyanka were already present at the airport. We reached home directly from the airport.

This beautiful city is situated on the banks of the Valtava River in the shade of natural valleys.

During my stay here, I got a chance to see and understand the entire city and its people including the beautiful Old Town, Museum, Dancing Building, Astronomical Clock built on medieval architectural style. It is also called the city of minarets.

The Czech Republic or Czechia (Czech: CESKO) is a country in the continent of Europe. Its capital is Prague.

Czechoslovakia was founded after World War I by two separate ethnic groups, Czechs and Slovaks, but after World War II, the region became part of Soviet power and was ruled by the Czechoslovakian Communist Party. The Velvet Revolution led to the transformation of 41 years of unilateral Communist Party rule into a parliamentary republic in 1989 and on 1st January 1993, the non-violent partition of

Czechoslovakia, the Czech Republic and Slovakia got established. The Czech Republic has a multi-party parliamentary democratic system in which the president is the head of state and the prime minister is the head of government. The parliament consists of the Chamber of Deputies and the Senate.

The author with fellow passengers at Prague airport

The behavior of the Czechs is friendly

Czechs are outspoken. There is a sense of patriotism among the people here. Respect for the country and priority of domestic products over foreign products in purchasing is in their nature. The people here are hard-working. Exercise, jogging and walking are in their daily routine. Their language is Czech. Czech is a Slavic language of the Western Slavic group, which includes Polish and Slovak. Natives of Czechs tend to keep a distance from new acquaintances until they know and understand them well. Generally, their behavior shows friendly and warmheartedness. They do not lag behind in the formality of greetings. When face-to-face, they used to say "Dobre Den", which means good day. At first I had difficulty in responding, but later I also responded to the other person's greeting by saying "Dobre Den". While getting off the metro or tram, the hitchhikers sitting next to him say "Nashle danou", which is also responded by "Nashle danou". "Nashle danou" means "good bye".

Charles Bridge over the Baltava River in Czech capital Prague

One day in the evening, I got a chance to go to a picnic spot on the banks of the river Valtava. It was 8:30 pm, but it wasn't sunset. Right now it sunsets here at around 8.48 pm. A crowd of tourists had gathered on the platform from Vuton to Old Town on the river bank. Some tourists were enjoying snacks and beer in restaurants or boat hotels on the platform, while some were busy boating. Apart from all this, there were also musical instruments and dance and music troupes in small groups. Everyone was enjoying this pleasant atmosphere.

Beautiful view of the Waldstein garden in Prague

No dirt anywhere on the roads

Unemployment is negligible here. These people come out of their homes dressed in full attire. The living conditions of the people, the rich housing system and the climate are testimony to the perfection of prosperity here. Everyone has the power of housing, car, money and food. Simple comforts are enough for them. This thinking reduces nervousness and stress in their lives. There is no trace of theft, snatching or any kind of crime here. There is no encroachment or dirt anywhere on the roads. There is a system of garbage bins at a distance, which is used by all. The behaviour of the police is friendly. People here are aware of following the law/rules. The city's traffic is quite smooth. Buses, trams and metro services are operated under public transport. There is a good system of public transport in the entire city, so that the common man does not have any inconvenience in traffic even without a car. Uber and Bolt's online booking service for taxis is available.

Europe Tour - 2 (Czech Republic)

Education is a priority of the Czech government.

Education is a priority for the Czech government. Children are usually sent to playschool after one year of age.

At the age of 6, they are enrolled in grade-1. Early education is free for Czech children. Higher education is also provided free in the Czech language. Education in English medium is not given free here, but it is expensive.

Children go to school by bus and tram. For this, they are trained.

Students have to leave home from the age of 16. Even if the child is living with the guardian, there is an obligation to pay the house rent. From student life, Czech youth start earning extra money through part-time work.

This gives an opportunity to try and understand oneself in various professions on the one hand, while on the other hand, there is enough money for daily expense and studies.

The practice of joint family is almost non-existent here. The younger generation here prefers to stay in relationships rather than marriage. Even after marriage, the process of divorce and remarriage with boyfriend continues. In the case of parents, divorce and subsequent marriages are often seen.

The principle of equality between men and women prevails.

Heritage of Prague: Astronomical clock in a magnificent ancient building

Equality also prevails in budget management and payment of bills. Usually, couples and families account for half of all expenses. There is a lack of enthusiasm among couples to have a child. People often keep a dog or cat as a compensation for not having children. Hardly anyone has more than two children, while the government has made a provision to create awareness among the citizens to increase the population, giving them special tax exemptions and other facilities.

The Narodni Museum in Prague

Here, people do their own household chores including sweeping, cleaning utensils, cooking and other household chores. There is no separate house help for this work. This is probably the reason why people here do not like to cook at home. They eat lunch at the restaurant and pack dinner when they return from office. Even in restaurants, these people do not share their food with each other. They eat food based on their orders. Non Vegetarian is preferred in food and beer in drinks. The reason for this is probably the cold weather here. In winter, the temperature here goes down to minus 20 degrees, while in summer it is a maximum of 30 degrees. Today (23rd May 2025), sunrise here was 05.04 am and sunset was 20.54 pm i.e. the day is still about 16 hours.

No sign of religious fanaticism

The Czech Republic is one of the least religious countries in Europe. Religion is dying here. There is no religious fanaticism at all. Most people consider themselves to be nonreligious or secular, which means not to bind or separate themselves from the traditions and beliefs of a particular religion. This shift in religious identity has come about since the second half of the 20th century. Earlier, more than 90 percent of the people here were Christians. This is probably the result of the 41-year history of communist rule.

9,000 Indian youth working in Prague

About 9,000 Indian youths work in various multinational companies in Prague, the capital of the Czech Republic. Due to the warmth, friendly attitude of the people here, labor-led laws and positive cooperative activities of the Indian Embassy, the Indian youth working here do not face any kind of problem. The Indian Embassy sponsors a variety of events on Indian festivals, in which Indians working here participate. India's relations with former Czechoslovakia and the present Czech Republic have always been cordial and friendly.

A visit to the Czech Republic is considered incomplete without a visit to the international film festival venue "Karlovy Vary", which is full of natural beauty. Therefore, my younger son Shiv Pratap and daughter-in-law Priyanka have scheduled a tour of Karlovy Vary on May 26, Italy from May 28 to June 2 and Austria, Germany and Switzerland in mid-June.

Europe Tour – 3 (Czech Republic)

The city of multi-storey buildings

It would not be an exaggeration to call Prague a city of multistorey buildings, because nowhere is there a building of less than four floors in addition to the ground floor. Almost all multi-storeyed buildings have only one main gate for entry and exit. Nowhere was there a government or private security guard at the main entrance. Almost all buildings have a sensor-based computerized lock on the main door, the censored key of which is available with all tenants and flat owners as well as the post office. Everyone uses their own sensor key to enter and exit the building. The entry and exit of the vehicle is also through the main entrance. It is parked in the basement and parking on the ground floor.

The names of all tenants and flat owners are written on the letter box inside the main entrance of the building. On receiving a letter or parcel, the post office staff enters the building by opening the main door with their censored key and returns by dropping the letter or parcel in the letter box of the person concerned. There is no guard or personnel available for parking even in malls or any big marketing complex. Drivers park their vehicles by depositing the parking amount in the parking machine. There was no boundary wall in the apartments anywhere. Every house is connected to the road and the main entrance of the house is connected to the footpath on the road. The side walls of all the buildings are adjacent to each other, perhaps there is no custom or legal requirement to leave a vacant space on the side of the house.

Prague,the city of multi -storey buildings

As per the pre-scheduled program, on May 26, we visited the famous international film festival venue "Karlovy Vary", full of natural beauty, spa therapy. I was accompanied by my wife Nirmala Singh, son Shiv Pratap and daughter-in-law Priyanka.

Beautiful view of the city of Karlovy Vary

The city of Karlovy Vary in the Czech Republic is one of Europe's tourist attractions. It is a beautiful city in the lap of nature located at a distance of 123 kilometers from the capital Prague . The entire slope of the rolling hills is covered with tall buildings carved on medieval architectural style, lush green plants and gardens of small blooming flowers from top to bottom. Its lush green peaks and enchanting climate are like paradise, which gives a feeling of unparalleled natural beauty. The clouds add to its beauty. This is the reason why every year the "Karlovy Vary International Film Festival" is organized here. Hindi - Nepali film "Ralang Road" was selected for the Crystal Award at the 52nd International Film Festival. The film was shot in Ralang city of Sikkim. The story is about a small mountain town. The film promotes cultural lifestyle in the social system. The 58th International Film Festival of India (IFFI) competition held here also included the Indian film "Santosh", directed by Sandhya Suri and starring Shahana Goswami and Sunita Rajwar.

Natural landscape of karlovy vary

Patients are treated in spa homes

There is also a hot water spring, which makes its nature of beauty enchanting. Due to being a cold region, people's attraction towards hot water is natural. The hot water of the spring is a blend of natural minerals. It is mainly used in spa therapy. That is why there is a sufficient number of spa houses where patients are treated. The hot water of the spring

Karlovy vary city nestled in the lap of nature

is an important part of the spa treatment. The full development of this city took place in the Soviet era. Even today, the population of Russians is more than Czechs.

There is a canal for the drainage of water from the hot spring. On both sides of the canal there is a footpath and a wide road platform for the convenience of tourists to roam around, following which the International Film Festival Center is located on foot, many boutiques, gift shops, spa medical houses, thermal spring, regional museum, grand hotel, hot spring, cafe, restaurants etc.

Europe Tour-4 (Florence, Italy)

Italy is a land of cultural heritage.

As per the earlier schedule, on May 28, 2025, at 5.50 am., the 6 days Italy tour started from my son's residence in Prague. The journey is managed by my son Shiv Pratap and daughter-in-law Priyanka. I am accompanied by my wife Nirmala Singh. We took Bolt cab to Prague airport. The driver of the cab was a Ukrainian. Tactfulness and warmheartedness were in his nature.

Ukrainian driver's spilled pain in conversation While the conversation started driver's started asking questions.

Question: Where are you all from?

Answer: We are all from India.

Qquestion: How safe are you all there?

Answer: We are all safe in India.

When asked, the driver said that I am from Ukraine. I was not safe there. I am in the Czech Republic and working in the Bolt cab service to earn a living. Due to the acceptance of the European Union, asylum has been found in the countries of Europe. Because of my old connections, I have made the Czech Republic my haven. The pain of external and internal insecurity of his country Ukraine was clearly visible on his face. In the course of the conversation, we had all reached Prague Airport. At the airport, passengers are allowed to go from the entrance to the boarding pass counter along with their family members. After boarding pass and security check, we boarded the Spanish Airlines flight. The plane arrived in Florence at 9.45 am.

Florence, the main center of tourist attraction

Florence is the most beautiful city in Italy as well as the main center of tourism. The city is famous for its rich history, distinct cultural heritage, museums, excellent art galleries, historical sites, architecture, etc.

Florence Cathedral of 13th century

Florence was a center of architecture and painting in the Italian Renaissance. Even today, there is a substantial number of painters painting/sketching around the Florence Cathedral and Square in the Old Town. They have mastered the art of making the exact picture by sitting in front of the person. Many magnificent buildings of the city such as Palazzo Pitti, Florence Cathedral, Basilica Church etc. are testimony to the rich architecture. Promoting art and culture has become the nature of the people here. The Florence Cathedral, built in the 13th century, is a magnificent example of excellent architecture. Its artistic facade, huge red dome, grand decoration of intricate marble and craftsmanship are incomparable. Basilica Church is a beautiful church built in the 14th century. The carvings of its facade are a unique example of superb craftsmanship.

This city is situated on the banks of the Arno River. There are many bridges on this river for ease of traffic. The Ponte Vexio Bridge is ancient, also known as the medieval stone bridge. The jewelry market and buildings built on this bridge are the centers of tourist attraction. The bridge has been closed for traffic. The traffic system here is smooth and restrained. In addition to public transport, trams and buses, private cab services are also available. The metro facility isn't here.

Crowd of tourists at a tourist spot in Florance

Also famous for the textile industry

The city is situated amidst the lush green valleys of mountain ranges, which add to its natural beauty. Piazzale Michelangelo is a charming place located at the top of the city, where tourists enjoy the panoramic and wonderful view of the sunset. Florence is also famous for its delicious cuisine. Olive oil, gelato ice cream and Tuscany wine are wonderfully used in local ingredients and products. Due to its health benefits, food items are usually prepared in olive oil. Florence has a long cultural tradition of skilled leather workmanship. Bags, belts, jackets, and other high-quality accessories have been made by artisans here for centuries. Florence also has a reputation for the textile industry.

The streets connected to Florence Cathedral are lined with pavement shopkeepers run by immigrants. These immigrants were once granted asylum by the Italian government. There is no trace of snatching, robbery and criminal incidents in the city, but pickpocketing and theft at the tourist place cannot be ruled out. The main reason for this is the illegal immigrants living here.

Reginal train at Florence railway station, Italy

Europe Tour- 5 (Pisa, Italy)

Galileo's birthplace fascinated

The famous tourist destination "Pisa" was one of the destination for excursion on 29th May'2025 in Italy. After leaving the hotel, we reached Florence railway station at 10 o'clock by tram. There is a market complex in the station premises, in which there are many shops of essential consumer goods like restaurants, medicine shops, book stalls etc. The station was crowded with tourists, but there was no panic due to the strong computerized information system of arrival and departure information of trains. Permission to go to the platform is allowed only after the departure information of the trains is displayed on the display board. Florence station has a total of 19 platforms (1A to 18).

Despite the plethora of trains and the rush of tourists, no one is inconvenienced. We all boarded the regional train to Pisa. The train reached Pisa in 55 minutes, after stopping at all its scheduled stops . The distance from Florence to Pisa is 99 kilometers. Each coach had a computerised display board inside the train, which displayed information about the temperature (inside and outside) of the coach, the next station and the speed of the train. All the coaches of the train are connected to each other from the inside and are airconditioned. One can also go inside a moving train in a coach. The maximum speed of the train here is 160 kilometers per hour. After reaching Pisa railway station, we reached the Leaning Tower complex by public transport "bus".

Leaning Tower of Pisa built in 1372 The tower here is famous as the "Leaning Tower of Pisa". The construction of this tower started in 1172 AD, which was completed in 1372 AD. Due to the proximity of the center of gravity of the tower, the leaning tower does not fall. Its height is 55.86 meters. The leaning tower of Pisa, made up of beautiful marble, is a masterpiece of architecture and a marvel of human intelligence. In the precincts of the Leaning Tower, the Pisa Cathedral, the Caposanto Graveyard, the Sinopie Museum, the Baptistery and the Opera del Duamo Museum are located, which make the entire complex attractive and beautiful. Here this premise is also called the wondrous ground of buildings.

Leaning Tower of Pisa

The grandeur of the Pisa Cathedral Church and the beautiful carvings and paintings on its walls are wonderful confluence of rich architecture and paintings. The grandeur, artistic carvings and paintings of the bapastry located in the premises are exquisite. It is pertinent to mention here that the conversion of people of other religions to Christianity started with a practice called Baptism and the place where this ceremony takes place is called Baptistry. That is, the conversion of people of other religions to Christianity has been a part of the working style of Christianity since ancient times. There was a good rush of tourists today. Everyone was making their journey memorable by capturing the panoramic view of the Leaning Tower and the surroundings in their cameras.

Pisa cathedral in the Leaning Tower complex

Situated on the Arno River, this city is historically and culturally very important. It is also the birthplace of the great scientist Galileo, the father of modern physics. Pisa is a name that is associated with a unique heritage of history, art and

Baptistery building in Pisa

engineering. Pisa is not only known for its leaning minaret, but also its picturesque streets, amazing cathedrals, and ancient university buildings reflect its rich cultural heritage.

The smell of art in the air

Every corner of Pisa is filled with the echo of history—the air here smells of art, the streets are filled with stories of centuries, and every brick in the tower bears witness to a new era. This place is not just a trip but also a touristic experience.

The public transport and traffic signaling system of the city of Pisa is very beautiful. Traffic personnel were not seen at any traffic post, but it did not affect the ease of traffic. There is also a separate signal lamp on the zebra cross for pedestrians. Pedestrians cross the road only when the light of the lamp is green. It is in the conduct of the people here to follow the traffic rules.

The city is also not far behind in the industrial sector. Pisa is also known as a production center for railway materials, motorcycles, bikes, cotton fabrics, glass, pottery, medicines and matches. We wandered around the Leaning Tower enclosure all day and returned back to Florence by the double-decker local train in the evening.

Europe Tour – 6 (Venice, Italy)

The City of Shakespeare's 'The Merchant of Venice'

As a student, I had heard about Venice which is situated in Italy . In those days, Shakespeare's books were taught in schools. In the same sequence, information was given about many books written by William Shakespeare, including the play "The Merchant of Venice". In fact, this book is a play based on the city of Venice. Shakespeare may have placed Venice at the centre of his book because of its adaptation to exploring such diverse subjects as commerce, race, religion, and marriage. Venice was, in any case, a city with cosmopolitan nature, a prosperous trading centre and an impressive port. Shakespeare often chose Italy for his plays, especially comedies, and Venice may have been an attractive choice for him. As soon as I arrived in Italy, the pent-up desire to visit Venice was ignited. Finally, with the consent of all, the tour of Venice was decided.

We arrived at Florence railway station in the morning to go to Venice on 30th May 2025. The seat on the train was already reserved. The journey to Venice began by train. All the coaches of the train are air-conditioned and are connected to each other from inside. There are three categories of train coaches, fare and facilities are also according to the categories. The three categories are known by different names i.e. Standard, Premium and Business. The maximum running speed of the train is 260 kilometers per hour. The distance from Florence to Venice is 271 kilometers. The train took one hour and fifty-five minutes to reach Venice from Florence, stopping at its scheduled halt. Here, passengers use the underpass to go from one platform to another.

Venice means the floating city

Venice is a beautiful and important city in Italy. Due to the abundance of canals and bridges, it is also called the city of canals and bridges. It is also known as the "floating city" due to its settlement on small sea islands. Built on 118 small islands, this city is a quintessential natural gift of architectural beauty. It is connected to hundreds of bridges and winding canals. The city is also historically and culturally important. The city has been declared as a World Heritage Site by UNESCO.

Venice, Italy: Gondola boat ride in the floating city

Venice is an attractive and popular tourist destination in Europe. The number of Christians is the highest here, but the presence of Muslims cannot be denied. Millions of tourists visit this place every year. The Gondola is an emblem of

Venice. Boating by gondola boat in the canals is the first choice of tourists. Saint Martin's Square, the Rialto Bridge and many museums are also tourist places here to visit.

The carved multi-storeyed buildings and curved bridges near the Rialto Bridge and Saint Martin's Square are the epitome of excellent architecture. The artistic decoration of the permanent restaurants, hotels, bars, ice creams, boutiques, gift items, footwear, fashion, jewelry etc. located at the foot of the buildings is the center of attraction for the tourists. The different groups of tourists boating in the canals with Gandola boats / motor boats are enough to enhance the glow of its natural beauty. The Saint Martin's Square complex itself has a museum preserved with other valuable heritage like minaret, cathedral, museum, grand shopping complex etc. The artistic paintings of marble carved figures on the walls of the Cathedral are indeed a unique example of the blending of excellent architecture and painting. Locals said that it is lavishly decorated in the Christmas festival. A large crowd of devotees gathers here. The weddings of the people of Venice are celebrated here with pomp. The beauty of the minaret, the artistic carvings of the walls of the museum and the grandeur of the market complex make the beauty of the entire complex enchanting.

Good system of public water transport

Private motor boats and motor boats operated by public water transport are available to move from one island to another. Public water transport is quite organized.

The Building at St. Martin's square

Almost all the islands have stations for the stoppage of motor boats. All stations have a centrally computerized display board, on which all the information related to the arrival and departure of the motor boat is continuously displayed. Adequate staff are posted at these stations for passenger facilitation. There is also a provision of boat ambulance with medical staff for medical emergencies. After taking tickets at Piazzale Roma Ghat to go to Murano Island, we all boarded the motor boat of Public Water Transport. We arrived at Murano in about half an hour.

Saw the process of glass manufacturing in the glass factory

Murano is a major center of glass production. Glass carvings and artistic gifts and decorations are also prepared here. Shiv Pratap had already booked the passes online on May 31st , 2025, at 2 pm to watch the glass manufacturing process at the Elegy Murano Glass Factory. At the appointed time, we all went to the glass factory and saw the whole process of glass making. In the hot furnace, there was an opportunity to get a glimpse of the art of getting the desired shape by molding the transparent liquid material of glass into different types of artistic molds. A glass jug and a horse were made and shown to all of us as a demonstration. From here we all went to Burano Island by public water transport boat. Burano is also famous for glass production. The colours of Venetian buildings are usually cream, yellow and brown, but Burano's story is different. The buildings here are colorful, which is the center of natural attraction for tourists.

The unique beauty of the islands fascinates the mind

There are many islands here, including Torcello, Isola de Saint Michael, Lido di Venezia, etc. All the islands have their own heritage story, but all the islands are equally adorned on the ground floor of multi-storey buildings built on advanced architectural style on both sides of the canals, restaurants, hotels, bars, ice cream, decorative items, toiletries, fashion, artistic gift shops, etc. Tourists stroll on the footpath between buildings and canals, a beautiful series of artistic bridge connecting the winding canals and groups of tourists boating in Gondola boats/motor boats in the canals. The unique natural beauty of all the islands looks like art paintings, attracting tourists to come here themselves.

After visiting Burano Island, we again boarded the motor boat of Public Water Transport to return to Saint Martin's

Square. The boat reached Saint Martin's Square in Venice in an hour and a half, stopping at all the scheduled stops. By then it was seven o'clock in the evening. The entire area of Saint Martin's Square was flooded with tourists. Everyone seemed to be enjoying their activities. Enjoying snacks and beer in a restaurant/hotel or shopping in a marketing complex or enjoying while boating or diving into the ocean of bliss in small groups in the area to the tune of music. There was a sense of happiness and joy on everyone's face. As a result, it was a very picturesque view.

Europe Tour – 7 (Verona, Italy)

City of Romeo and Juliet

During a visit to Venice, it was found that Verona is a major tourist destination and William Shakespeare's famous play "Romeo and Juliet" is based on the story of two lovers of Verona. I had heard about Shakespeare's Romeo-Juliet when I was a student, as a result of which the desire to visit his city "Verona" was strengthened and accordingly the next program was also scheduled. We arrived at Venice railway station in the morning to go to Verona on 1st June 2025.

There is a market complex in the station premises, in which restaurants, book stalls, medical shops and shops of all essential materials are available.

Italo, Italian fast train

The journey to Verona began by double-decker train. Each coach has a computerized display board inside and outside. It is a common protocol to give information about the train number, coming station, temperature of the bogie and the speed of the train to the passengers along with the advertisement by the display board inside the coach. The display board also has a camera, in which the view of the passengers sitting in the bogie is also displays and the train number and its destination are displayed by the display board outside the coach as well. All the coaches of the train are airconditioned and connected to each other from inside. The maximum running speed of the regional train is 160 kilometers per hour. The distance from Venice to Verona is 115 kilometers. The train took one hour and three minutes to reach Verona from Venice, stopping at its scheduled stops. There is no overbridge anywhere at the railway station, but there is an underpass everywhere. Passengers use underpasses only to move from one platform to another.

Verona is an important city in the northern region of Italy. It is situated on the banks of the second longest river in Italy "Aedes". It is famous for its history, art, culture and Shakespearean connection. Here Verona Arena, Pietra Bridge, Cathedral, Museum, Clock Tower, Old Town Square, Juliet's House, grand buildings built on beautiful architectural style and shopping complexes are centers of tourist attraction. The city is marked as a World Heritage Site by UNESCO.

Verona Arena- The Oldest Roman Arena

The Verona Arena, built in the 1st century, is one of the oldest Roman amphitheaters. It was built during the reign of Emperor Octavian Augustan. The Verona Arena is not only an ancient monument, but it is an important part of Verona's identity and cultural heritage and an example of the creative passion of human beings. Starting with the Gladier Games from its inception, it has now established itself as a world famous opera house. Today the Verona Arena is known for its Summer Opera Festival.

The oldest amphitheatre of Verona Arena

The Pietra Bridge is one of Verona's most iconic and historic landmarks. It is also called a stone bridge. Marble and stone materials have been used in its construction. This is a very ancient bridge. The engineering and architecture of its design is not only fascinating, but also the identity of Verona's cultural heritage. This bridge is built on the Eddies River.

The castle of Castelvecchio was built by the Della Scala family, also known as Scaligeri, during their reign. It is a fortified palace built on a stunning medieval architectural style. Being situated on a hill covered with natural beauty, it looks quite beautiful. It has impressive museums, Scaligeri tombs, Piazaa dei Signori and monuments. The beautiful artistic architectural style of multi-storeyed buildings in the Old Town Square complex, grand shopping complexes, graceful clock towers, built on artistic carved style are the natural reasons for the attraction of the church. With modern amenities, comfortable public transport and a rich cultural landscape, the quality of life is elevated.

Juliet's house creates thrill

Two plays written by William Shakespeare "Romeo and Juliet" and "The Two Gentle Men of Verona" are centered around Verona, but the play "Romeo and Juliet", based on the story of two lovers, has more influence on tourists. The house of Juliet provides the real link to the literary world. The balcony of this 14th -century building resembles the balcony where Juliet used to stand when Romeo expressed love. The courtyard under the balcony is full of visitors. A bronze statue of Juliet is installed in this courtyard. There is a crowd of tourists to take their selfies with the bronze statue for their good luck. There is a competition among the tourists to take their selfie with the bronze statue first. It is a very picturesque view. Some tourists were seen locking the premises to fulfill their wishes. There were already a lot of locks there. Romeo and Juliet may not be real people, but they are immortal characters in literature.

Casa de Julieta means Juliet's house. The house has nine rooms. It has been converted into a well-equipped museum. The museum exhibits separate Veronese style murals from the 13th to the 19th century, 19th century paintings related to the story of two lovers, ceramic objects from the Middle Ages and the early Veronese Renaissance, from the film adaptation of Franco Zeffirelli to furniture and costumes of the period. This house museum of the Romantic period was renovated by the city of Verona in 2004. During the renovation, the original form of the medieval facade made of unplastered bricks came to the fore, which has become the center of attraction at present.

Thousands of heart-shaped locks are installed in Juliet's house premises. People consider it a symbol of good luck

The main problem during migration is of lodging and food, which had already been solved by son Shiv Pratap and daughter-in-law Priyanka. Based on the booking, we used to stay in flats operated under the Airbnb app, where there is a cooking arrangement. The app is global, but its prevalence in India is low. In Italy, Indian food is not available other than Indian restaurants, but Indian restaurants have a presence in major cities. We all just used to eat lunch at Indian restaurants. Breakfast and dinner were prepared in the flat for the rest of the time.

Europe Tour - 8 (Italy)

Most World Heritage Sites in Italy

I have returned to Prague after finishing my 6-day stay in Italy. The trip to Italy was a pleasant and memorable one for me. Italy has the distinction of being the country with the most World Heritage Sites, because 58 of the World Heritage Sites declared by UNESCO are in Italy alone. I had the opportunity to see four of these cities, Florence, Pisa, Venice and Verona, and their World Heritage Sites, which I have already mentioned.

Italy is an attractive and touristy country of South Europe located in the Mediterranean Sea. It's language is Italian and currency is Euro. Rome, a city with a rich cultural heritage, is its capital. The historical area of Rome is also marked as a World Heritage Site by UNESCO.

This historical area is a mixture of monuments and buildings of different eras. Italy is the sixth largest country in Europe in terms of population and the tenth largest country in terms of area. Prosperity and affluence are in the climate here. It is the world's eighth largest economy and the third largest in the euro world. Italy is famous for its contributions to fashion, art, architecture, opera, literature, design and film.

Politically, after a referendum on 2nd June 1946, the monarchy in Italy was transformed into a democratic republic. On January 1st, 1948, the Constitution was adopted and the parliamentary democratic system was accepted, due to which the people exercise their power through their elected representatives in the Parliament.

The Italian Parliament has a bicameral system, including the Chamber of Deputies and the Senate of the Republic. It is elected every five years by voters of eighteen or older. Voters 25 years of age or older are eligible to become deputy electors and voters 40 or older are eligible to become senators. The election of senators from each region is based on a system of proportional representation. **Catholic makes 75% of Italy's population**

The religious history of Italy begins with the Roman Empire, which was a polytheist. Christianity later spread to Rome and it became the Catholic state religion, but Italy became a secular state with the amendment of the Constitution in 1948 and the Lateran Treaty in 1984. That is, the guarantee of freedom of religion became certain. However, the Catholic Church still plays an important role in Italian society and politics. Catholics makes about 75 percent of Italy's population. Apart from this, people of Protestant, other Christianity, Islam, Hinduism, Buddhism and Judaism also live here. There are some people who do not believe in the beliefs and traditions of any religion, that is, they have not associated themselves with any religion.

The main food here is pasta, pizza, cannoli and pastries. Lunch is the main meal, which lasts one and a half to two hours. Common Italian lunches include primo (pasta, soup or risotto dish) and secondo (a dish made of meat or fish). Italians do not throw away leftover food, but they have an incredible talent to make from leftover food something new and tasty again. Their dinner is lighter than lunch, which is eaten by 8 o'clock, so that digestion can be better and good sleep can be achieved. Along with food, these people like wine & beer.

Unlike in the Czech Republic, the joint family system has not been completely abolished, as evidenced by the presence of

Italians enjoying family tours at tourist destinations.

Venice- A City in Italy, located on the Sea Islands

Education compulsory for children from 6 to 16 years

Education is a priority for the Italian government. According to the age of the children, the education system here is determined in five phases. There are nursery schools for children between 3 to 5 years of age, primary schools for children between 6 to 11 years of age, middle schools for children between 11 to 14 years, higher secondary schools for children between 14 to 19 years of age and colleges and universities for higher education. Education is compulsory for children between the ages of 6 to 16 in Italy. At each level, an examination is held at the end of the year, which is necessary to attain the degree and reach the next degree of education. There are public and private education systems. Education in Italy is given in the Italian language, but many universities allow education in English language as well. Public education is free for all children living in Italy, regardless of their nationality. The course also emphasizes art and culture, which are an integral part of Italy's heritage.

A developed economy of the European Union

As a byproduct of the Second World War, people have seen Italy transform from an agrarian economy to an advanced country of the world. Italy's economy is a strong and developed economy of the European Union. Italy's position in the production of automobiles, fashion, machinery and electronics is quite strong. Cotton, wool, coal and chemicals are imported here and fruits, yarn, clothes, machines, motor vehicles, food items, tobacco, motorcycles, etc. are exported from here. Italy's agricultural sector is also very strong, due to which there is good farming. In the northern region of Italy corn, rice, sugar beet, soybeans, meat, fruits and dairy products are mainly produced, while in the southern region wheat, olives etc. Italy also counts as a producer of highquality wine.

There is no trace of criminal incidents like theft, snatching, pickpocketing, cheating in Italy. The incident of pickpocketing in a crowded place just around a tourist spot cannot be ruled out, mainly due to illegal infiltrators living

Juliet Balcony, Verona, Italy

here. In special circumstances, immigrants were given shelter here earlier, after which illegal infiltrators also entered here. Well, the people here are very nice. They are kind and open-minded. Their behavior is positive. Respecting each other is ingrained in their behavior, but young couples are often seen expressing love to each other in parks or public places. Sometimes, the pair transcends all limits of decorum, which is called vulgarity in Indian culture and openness in Western culture.

The Old Town Square is the same among all the cities of Italy, where there are churches, clock towers, museums, multi-storey buildings and shopping complexes, built on excellent architectural style, which have been developed from the point of view of tourism. Traffic is smooth and orderly within all the cities. Buses and trams are operated under public transport. The entire traffic system is computerized, so that tourists get information about the transport schedule on mobile. The option to buy a ticket for a public transport journey is also available on mobile. There is a computerized display board at all the stoppages. Vehicular traffic information is displayed, which does not cause any inconvenience to the passengers.

Relationship between India and Italy is old

Like India, Italy is also counted among the historical countries. It also has the largest number of historical sites and the agriculture sector is one of the priorities of the government. In this way, Italy and India have in common in many respects. The relationship between India and Italy is very old. The positive chemistry between Prime Minister Maloney of Italy and Prime Minister of India at the G20 meeting held under the chairmanship of India last year has strengthened this relationship considerably.

Now the next stop is Austria, Germany and Switzerland, which will start on June 15th and end on June 21st.

Europe Tour – 9 (Rothenburg & Fussen, Germany)

Multi-storey buildings The beauty of Rothenburg

On 15th June 2025, at 9 am, we started our journey to Germany by road. Shiv Pratap has rented the Skoda car for a week and is also driving. He has a driving license here. On the highway of the Czech Republic, the speed limit is 130 kilometers per hour, but the maximum speed limit is not there as soon as we enter the German border. There is a Waze app all over Europe for navigation. This app not only guides the direction of the destination, but also the speed set by the government, the speed of the vehicle, lane information, the vehicle standing ahead on the road and the information related to construction work comes with an alert on the screen. The alarm automatically indicates even when the speed of the vehicle increases from the prescribed speed. The highway in Germany is toll free.

There is constant greenery on both sides of the highway. There is a crop in the fields. The greenery of the crop is a sign of advanced agriculture. Wind turbines and large-scale solar panels are installed at various places to get wind and solar energy from nature, which shows the commitment of the German government towards renewable energy. At 12:30 in the afternoon, we arrived in the ancient tourist city of Rothenburg in Germany. The distance from Prague to Rothenburg is 385 kilometers.

Rothenburg is the ancient city of Germany. The town is situated on the Tauber hill. The entire hill is covered with greenery and its innate natural beauty is the center of attraction. Multi-storeyed buildings built of stone and wood on the medieval artistic style are the beauty of this city. All the houses in the city are connected by road. There is pavement on both sides of the road. Restaurants, hotels, shops adorning apparel, jewellery, gift items, etc. in the buildings adjacent to the pavement add to the brightness of the city. Footpaths and ròads are made only of stone and coball stone.

The city is protected by a fortified high wall. It is quite enjoyable to walk on it. Tourists get lost in the scenic view of the valley while taking a walk. Tourists throng to see the cathedral with carved figures. Apart from European countries, there are also tourists from South Korea, Japan, America, India etc. The city has the highest number of Christians. The design of the watch tower is also a living testimony to medieval history.

Cycling or relaxing walks on the city wall make the trip memorable. The fortified walls of the city, the Tower Castle Gardens, the view of the Rothenburg Ob der Tower Castle Gate and the garden of Fitzinger Castle add to the beauty of this city. Medieval Crime Museum, Rothenburg Museum, Cathay Wohlffert Christmas Village, German Christmas Museum, St. Jacob's Tower, Fitzinger-Jacob Church etc. are the major tourist destinations, which are vivid evidence of the history of this city and give tourists a chance to immerse themselves in medieval history. Tourists can be seen laughing and having fun with delicious food and wine from cafes and restaurants.

Indian restaurant named Taj Mahal

There is also an Indian restaurant called Taj Mahal. Its director is Gopichand ji from Dehradun. He came here 25 years ago and now he lives here with his whole family. Only his mother lives in the village. During a comparative discussion on India and Germany, Gopichand said that health and education are free here, only higher education and research have a nominal fee. The government also gives a stipend for this. There are more employment opportunities available here. There is no practice of visiting offices and bribing for any work here. He also said that since Modiji has become the Prime Minister of India, progress is also being made over there.

Hotel Taj Mahal, Rothenburg, Germany

From Rothenburg we reached Altusried, which is 208 kilometers from Rothenburg. It is a village in Germany, bordering Austria and Switzerland. All types of civic amenities like electricity, water, gas, internet are available in the village. Each house is connected by a metalled road. Almost all the houses have a covered shed for car parking in front of the house and there is a small garden behind the house. There is a dustbin outside every house, in which garbage is dumped. Here all the household work, cutting the grass of the garden, maintenance of plants is done by the people of the house themselves. The standard of living of the villagers is of high standard, which is a reflection of the economic prosperity here. The two-room flat was booked for a week through the Airbnb app. Accommodation and cooking facilities are available in the flat. The rest of the journey to Austria, Switzerland and Germany is to be completed from here.

According to the schedule, on the second day, we reached Fussen by road. Fussen is a small town in Germany with a natural landscape nestled on the banks of lakes in the lap of the hills. It is located in the Rhine-Palatinate state of Germany, which is known for its historical sites, natural beauty, comfortable atmosphere and peace of mind.

Neuschwanstein Palace – A unique example of Architectural Marvel

King Ludwig II of Bavaria built the most famous palace, Neuschwanstein. This beautiful palace is a unique example of excellent architecture. The Neuschwanstein Castle, the Hohenschwangau Castle, the museum and the natural beauty of the Allgau region are the main attractions of this city. Neuschwanstein Castle is located on a hill above the city, while Hohenschwangau Castle is a neo-Gothic castle that was built in the 19th century.

Fussen is located in the Allgau region, known for its beautiful mountains, lakes, and lush pastures. The area is a popular destination for hiking, cycling, and other outdoor activities.

Author and his family members are witnessing Unique example of Neuschwanstein castle architecture in Fussen

Fussen is home to a number of art galleries and museums that reflect the city's cultural history. Fussen is also known for its local cuisine, including meat dishes, fish dishes, and local bakery products.

There are two lakes Alp and Forggen There is a substantial number of people boating and surfing in the lake. A pair of young and middle-aged tourists are lying on the lake shore in tight clothes for a sunbath. What we all call obscenity in Indian tradition, people here consider it a symbol of the openness of society. It's almost the same story of all lakes.

The natural beauty of the Zugspitze

Europe Tour- 10 (Germany)

Germany's political culture is vibrant.

Germany is a democratic country in Central Europe nestled between the Baltic Sea and the Alps hills. It is a member country of the European Union. Its economy is the largest in the European Union. It is known for its history, rich cultural heritage, geography and beautiful tourist places. Its capital is Berlin, which is Germany's most populous city. German is the official language here. The currency here is the Euro. Germany is bordered by Denmark to the north, Poland and the Czech Republic to the east, Austria and Switzerland to the south, France, Luxembourg, Belgium, and the Netherlands to the west.

Germany is a federal parliamentary republic. Its legislative powers are vested in the Bundestang (Parliament) and the Bundestrat (House of States' Representatives). The judiciary here is independent. The functions of the Executive and the Legislature are different. The political culture here is vibrant. People actively participate in political affairs and elect their representatives in free and fair elections. The lower house of the federal parliament elects the principal chancellor of the government. It has a multi-party polity. As in India, all citizens are equal before the law. Everyone has the right to expression. People can say what they think without hesitation. Everyone has the right to assemble and meet in groups. All citizens have the freedom to move and reside anywhere in the country as per their wish. The government system here is welfare. Under the social security system, medical care, unemployment compensation and other social needs are met by the government.

Eibsee, Germany - A panoramic view of lake Ebsee

All 16 states in Germany set their own education policies differently. Children between the ages of 6-7 attend primary school. Christian religious education is offered in most schools, but moral education is available as an alternative. Every child has the right to go to school. There are universities in the public and private sector in Germany.

Education is generally offered free at a public university, but is not free at private universities. It also has some of the best universities in the world like Technical University of Berlin, Heidelberg University etc. Football is a popular sport in Germany and many times Germany has also won the World Cup.

No bigotry on religious freedom

There is religious freedom in Germany. Everyone has the right to choose and practice their religion according to their choice. Most of the people here are Christians (Roman Catholic or Protestant). People of other religions also live here. According to the locals, one-fourth of the people here have no religion, that is, these people have not associated themselves with the established activities and traditions of any religion. There is absolutely no sense of religious fanaticism in the climate here. The number of nuclear families is increasing here. The joint family system is almost at an end. The people here are forthright and disciplined. Obeying the law and rules, punctuality and respecting each other's privacy are in the behavior of the people here. Criminal incidents like theft, snatching, pickpocketing etc. are negligible here.

There are many popular tourist destinations in Germany, including Berlin, Munich, Rothenburg, Fussen, Zugspitze, Ebsee, Heidelberg, Frankfurt, etc. Germany's beautiful natural scenery includes mountains, lakes, and forests. Bus and tram services are available under public transport in all cities. All the information including the arrival and departure of the bus and trams is computerized and displayed on the display board of each stoppage. The highway here is toll free and there is no speed limit for vehicles on the highway.

Global Leader of the Automobile Industry

There are a large number of production industries in Germany. Germany is a global leader of the automobile industry, with major companies such as Volkswagen, Mercedes-Benz, BMW and Audi. The engineering sector includes the production of machinery, appliances, pharmaceuticals in the chemical sector, agrochemicals, consumer electronics in the electronics sector, industrial electronics and telecommunication equipment. Germany is a major producer of electrical equipment. These include electrical machinery, appliances and other electrical products. Steel, aluminum and other base metals are also produced in Germany, along with the production of transport equipment, rail, ships and aircraft. Here tires, pipes, packaging and other materials are produced in rubber and plastic products.

Germany is also a leading country in the field of science and technology. It has made many important scientific discoveries. Germany has made great progress in the field of hydrogen fuel technological development. It has thus prepared the ground for playing a global role in the production and use of green hydrogen. Under this, Germany has developed a National Hydrogen Strategy, which aims to promote the production of green hydrogen and develop the technology of hydrogen fuel.

Hydrogen-powered trains

Hydrogen is a clean fuel option. Fuel produces only water after it is finished in the cell, which is a better option than CNG in terms of pollution. Germany already has hydrogenpowered trains in operation. This technology has emerged as an important option in the field of transportation. The hydrogen-powered car has two highly compressed and low compress tanks. Strong tanks and pipes are used because of the flammability of hydrogen gas. Under this technology, oxygen is passed from one side and hydrogen from the other side in the chamber. The chemical reaction between the two releases energy, which drives the car. It removes water instead of smoke, it does not cause pollution. This is why hydrogen fueling stations are being set up here, to fuel hydrogen-powered trains and other vehicles. Work is also being done in Germany on hydrogen fuel cell technology, which converts hydrogen into electrical energy. Wind turbines and solar panels have been installed on a large scale by the German government to obtain wind and solar energy from nature.

ICE-Intercity Express by DB(Deutsche Bahn) Germany

Climate change caused by carbon emissions is a major challenge for human civilization. Changes in weather patterns on the global stage, increase in the frequency of temperature and natural disasters are due to this. India along with the international community has also taken it seriously and is campaigning to limit carbon emissions and promote alternative energy sources like renewable energy and both countries are actively cooperating on renewable energy and Germany has also signed an agreement with the Government of India for cooperation in the development of green hydrogen technology.

Bilateral relations between India and Germany

Bilateral relations between India and Germany are based on shared democratic values. Germany is India's largest trading partner in Europe. The two countries cooperate on issues such as climate change, international terrorism and a stable global economic order. Both the countries within the G-4 group are supporters of reforms in the UN Security Council. Relations between the two countries have strengthened in economic, political and social spheres.

Europe Tour-11 (Innsbruck-Austria)

Innsbruck nestled in the foothills of the Alps

We arrived in Innsbruck at 10 am on 18th June 2025 by road. Innsbruck is an important city in Austria. It is located in the state of Tyrol. Nestled in the foothills of the Alps, this city has a natural cover of beauty. This Austrian city is full of natural beauty, has rich history and it's cultural heritage, is a major center of tourist attraction. The city is situated on the banks of these rivers. The Old Town of this city is also an important tourist destination due to its historical heritage and cultural heritage.

Innsbruck's old town square

The North of Innsbruck has a range of hills. Everyone wants to go to the top of the hill to see the panoramic natural landscape of the hills up close. Even we could not resist our strong desire to go to the top. There is a funicular and cable car to go to the top of the Innsbruck hill. Altstadt, Tirol, Alpanzoo, Hungerberg, Seagrube and Hefelekar are a total of six stops to reach the top peak. The journey to Hungerberg is arranged by funicular and the rest of the journey is done by cable car in two phases. A funicular is a type of rail system, which is used to carry passengers over mountains or steep slopes.

We arrived at Hungerberg by funicular. From here we all reached Hafelekar (the top of Innsbruck) by changing the stand from Seagrube and from Seagrube by another cable car. The view of the top peak is quite pleasant and enchanting. The natural landscape of the mountain range is unique, thrilling and enchanting. Everyone is busy capturing this scene on camera. There is a chance to get down at each stop and walk around to see the scenic beauty of the hills.

The Old Town Square of this city is also a popular tourist destination. The paintings and design of the multi-storeyed historical buildings here are quite attractive. These buildings have hotels, restaurants, cafes, jewelry, fashion, gift items. Roads and footpaths are made of coball stone. The buildings of watch towers, cathedrals and museums are also unique examples of exquisite architecture with carved figures. The city's fame is also due to its golden roof. The ceiling of a balcony of the multi-storey house in Old Town is studded with 2,657 gold leaves, this is called the golden roof. The artistic painting of this house is attractive. The royal church "Hofkirche" here is also worth visiting. This royal church has a monument to Emperor Maximilian and 38 marble statues. Ambras Castle on the outskirts of the city is a magnificent castle, with a museum and beautiful gardens. Bus and tram services are available in the city under public transport, which facilitates commuting within the city. All the stops are equipped with a computerized display board, on which all the information including the arrival and departure of the bus and tram is displayed.

The balcony roof, famously known as the Golden roof,is studed with 2657 gold leaves

Innsbruck is a popular destination for skiing in winter, with many ski resorts and slopes. Innsbruck has many more historical buildings and museums that showcase its rich cultural heritage. The description of Innsbruck is incomplete without Austria's knowledge. Therefore, it is necessary to know Austria.

Austria is a beautiful country located in Central Europe. It is bordered by eight countries such as Germany, Czech Republic, Slovakia, Hungary, Slovenia, Italy, Switzerland and Liechtenstein. It is no less than a paradise for tourists. Most of its area is covered with Alps hills, which makes its natural beauty incomparable and enchanting. There are a lot of tourists here in the summer period.

The head of government in Austria is the chancellor

Austria is a federal parliamentary republic with the head of government being the Chancellor and the head of state being the President. The Republic of Austria consists of nine states. Both regional and federal governments exercise executive power. On May 15th , 1955, the United States,

Great Britain, France and the Soviet Union ratified the Austrian State Treaty in Vienna, which led to the reestablishment of Austria as an independent and neutral state after its collapse. The Germans ruled this country for a long time. As a result, German civilization spread in Austria and the German language is spoken here. Vienna is its capital. Vienna is also the headquarters of the International Atomic Energy Agency (IAEA). The currency here is Euro and it is a member country of the European Union.

The best technique for tunneling in the mountains

Austria is a country with an advanced and developed capitalist economy. It ranks higher than many countries in terms of economic freedom. Technology, metals and machinery are the main components of industrial production. They have the best technique to tunnel in the mountains. Due to the hilly area, a lot of tunnels have been built here. This country is not far behind in terms of trade. It has trade with the European Union and other countries. Austria's service sector is large. Being a high-income country, the Gross Domestic Product (GDP) per capita is higher than many countries in the world. Agriculture is also an important sector, which contributes to food production. The government's economic policy aims to promote growth, innovation and employment.

The people of Austria are open-hearted.

The people here are open-hearted. Warm-heartedness is in their nature. There is no trace of criminal incidents here. All people discharge their civic duty. Their warmth with tourists is a living example of their lively lifestyle. Austria is quite a popular tourist destination for its beautiful landscapes, historic cities, and ski resorts. Being a democratic country, there is religious freedom in Austria. Everyone is allowed to behave in accordance with their religious beliefs. The largest part of the population, about 75 percent, profess Roman Catholicism. Apart from this, people of non-religious faith, Protestants, Muslims, Christians, people of Orthodox religion also live here.

Teaching in Austria is carried out by public, private and international schools. The education is in the German language. Secondary school education is compulsory for all children between the ages of 6 to 15. After nine years of compulsory education, young people can either continue schooling or join professional training till the age of 18. The educational level here is divided into primary, secondary and higher education. Austria is of great importance for the highest education of various disciplines. Vienna, Graz, Linz and Innsbruck are famous universities of the world. International students have the option of working and living in Austria after obtaining a bachelor's degree.

Health insurance mandatory for all

Healthcare in Austria is available to all residents and citizens of EU countries. Health insurance is compulsory here and can be obtained through the National Health Insurance Fund or private insurance. Students from the European Union or Switzerland who have their country's national health insurance can use the European Health Insurance Card. Free healthcare is provided to pensioners, spouses of workers, the unemployed and those unable to work due to other reasons.

India and Austria Strategic Partners

Bilateral relations between India and Austria have been strengthened. India played an important role in the negotiations with the Soviet Union in 1955 at the time of Austria's independence. India and Austria are strategic partners. Electronic goods, apparel, textiles, footwear, rubber goods, vehicles and railway parts are exported by India to Austria.

Two Austrian satellites, Tugsat-1/Bright and Unibright, were launched in 2013 from India's Satish Dhawan Space Centre, Sriharikota. Ayurveda and yoga have gained popularity in Austria and its capital. Vienna, is home to several schools of yoga.

Europe Tour-12 (Lucerne, Rhine Fall, Stein am Rhein, Zurich, Switzerland)

Wonderful Boating in Lake

On 19th June 2025 at about 9.30 am, we all reached Lucerne, Switzerland by road. Lucerne is a beautiful and prominent city of Switzerland as well as the capital of the Canton. The town may have been named " Lucerne" due to its location on the banks of the River Lursson. The city is known for its beauty, historical significance and natural scenery. There are many places of interest here, including the Chapel Bridge, the Lion Monument, Memorial and the historic Old Town. Lucerne is also identified as the center of Switzerland's tourism, culture and economy.

On both sides of Lucerne lake, there is a wide strip of cobble stone for tourists to visit and they have good seating arrangements. There are sufficient number of boats available for boating. Crowds of tourists can be seen enjoying boating throughout the day. There are also birds in the lake. In many places, groups of tourists are feeding these birds a piece of bread.

There are many bridges on the lake to go from one shore to the other, but the beauty of the Chapel Bridge is the main center of tourist attraction. This bridge is an ancient bridge made of wood. Its artistic shed is also wooden, there is a flower pot in a straight line on both sides of the shed, which adds to its beauty. Tourists queue up here for selfies and photography.

Ancient wooden chapel bridge over the Lursson river

Lion Memorial Historical Documents

The panoramic view of the greenery of Lake Lurssen and the surrounding uber-bayer hills is breathtaking. This view gives Lucerne fascinating natural beauty. The Lion Monuments, Memorial and the Old Town Square which was built in 1821, document the historical importance of the town. There are many museums, art galleries and theaters here, which are evidence of the cultural heritage of Lucerne.

Located in the Old Town of this city, the cathedral building is grand and attractive, built on an exquisite architectural style with carved figures. The artistic paintings inside the building are also quite beautiful and attractive. The multistorey buildings of the Old Town have currently been converted into shopping complexes. All buildings are connected by road. The Old Town has many museums, churches, watch towers, historical buildings, etc.

Tram and bus services are available under public transport for commuting in the city. Apart from this, there is also a private car service. Lucerne is a quiet and cozy city, offering tourists a pleasant experience. The lake, the Chapel Bridge and the grandeur of the historic old town and the area surrounding the lake are an ideal center for excursions.

Rhine Falls: An Attractive Tourist Destination

Rhine Falls, located near Lucerne, is an important tourist destination. Its distance from Lucerne is 101 kilometers. Its natural landscape is the center of attraction due to its location in the foothills. There is a kingdom of greenery all around. The roar of the waterfall of the Rhine Falls, the group of boating tourists and the rush to capture the beautiful scene in the cameras make the whole atmosphere beautiful.

There is a wide strip on the banks of the lake for tourists to walk. The entire strip is decorated with stone and coball stone. There is a bench to sit on. Trash cans are kept at small distances. There is a good system of boating here. In addition to the public boating service, private boats are also available for tourists. The boating ticket is obtained from the counter in cash or by card.

The boating time and boat number are marked on the ticket itself, so that tourists do not have to face trouble. We also enjoyed boating. When the boat reached close to the fall, the wobble of the boat, the roar of the waterfall, the happiness of the people sitting on the boat made the atmosphere thrilling with the water bath of the boat riders.

Artistic Painting on Wooden Buildings

We reached Stein am Rhein by road. It is 21 kilometers from Rhine Falls. This small ancient city of Switzerland is situated on the Rhine River. There are multi-storey wooden buildings on both sides of the road. The artistic paintings done on these buildings are quite attractive. These buildings have

Enchanting Natural beauty of Rhine Falls

restaurants, hotels, fashion, museum gift shops. There is a good number of tourists in the restaurant and coffee shops, all enjoying refreshments and wine. The behavior of the people here is cooperative. It would not be an exaggeration to say that this city belongs to Christians. There is a footpath adjacent to the buildings on both sides of the road. Only cobal stones have been used in footpaths and road construction. All buildings are connected to the street. The watch tower built on medieval architecture is the center of attraction. The buildings of the Cathedral and Museum with carved figures are unique examples of excellent architecture. The natural landscape of the foothills is enough to attract tourists. There are ample number of boats for boating in the river. There are a large number of tourists. Some are visiting the Old Town and some are enjoying boating. This city gives mental peace as well as realizing its natural beauty. It's 9 pm now. Tomorrow's event is in Zurich, which is located 54 kilometers from here .

'Dilwale Dulhania Le Jayenge' was shot in Zurich Zurich is counted among the beautiful cities of Switzerland. Zurich is a charming city situated on the banks of the lake. Its natural beauty is very attractive, due to which a lot of tourists come here. Due to its natural landscape, a lot of Indian films have been shot here, in which "Dilwale Dulhania Le Jayenge" is prominent.

The city is the capital of the canton of Zurich, Switzerland, as well as the country's most prominent industrial, trading, and banking city. It is the densest and most idyllic city in Switzerland. Most of it is made by drying the lake. The old part is still dense, but the new part has wide roads and beautiful buildings. The river Limmat divides the city into two parts. These two parts are connected to each other by 11 bridges.

Wonderful confluence of different cultures

The city's public transportation system is very good, making it easy to get around the city. There is compassion in the behavior of the people here. They are ready to help when we say something.

The city of Zurich has a rich history. Zurich has many museums, art galleries and theaters, which distinguish it as an ancient cultural center. Zurich is considered one of the best cities in the world due to the excellent lifestyle of the people here. People from different cultures and backgrounds live in Zurich, which makes this city special.

Lake Zurich, the Old Town, various museums, art galleries and the Alps hills on the horizon provide an atmosphere of paradise to the beauty of this city. Its luxurious spa, clean air, pollution-free nature and climate are important from physical health point of view.

The Most Beautiful Grossmunster Church

There are many major scenic ancient buildings, the most beautiful of which is the Grossmunster Church on the right bank of the Limmat River. There are 24 cosmic religious rules written on the walls of this church. Near the girls' schools in the vicinity are remnants of Roman architecture dating back to the 12th and 13th centuries. On the left bank of the Limmat is the Frau Muster, the second largest cathedral in Zurich, dating back to the 12th century. St. Peter's Church is the oldest. The Central Library had 700,000 books in 1916, where letters from famous social reformers and preacher Zwingli, Burliger, Lady Jane and Sheeler are preserved. There is also a statue of Zwingli installed in 1885. The National Museum is the grandest of the new buildings, which has a wonderful collection of all the arts and arts of Switzerland. The botanical garden here is one of the famous botanical gardens in the world. The city has factories for making silk and cotton textiles, machine parts, candles, soap, sugarcane, splatter, paper and leather materials.

A city that invites peace

Amidst the rich culture and delicious food, every area of this city invites peace. Zurich Airport is the largest international airport in Switzerland and a major hub for Swiss International Airlines. Zurich is the largest city in Switzerland and is famous for its cultural heritage and natural beauty. Lake Zurich, the natural beauty of the Alps and historical buildings attract tourists. The climate and lifestyle here reflect economic prosperity, due to which the quality of life here is high.

Stein am Rhien, Switzerland

Europe Tour – 13 (Switzerland)

Switzerland is the most beautiful country in the world.

A brief description of Switzerland is necessary to complete the discussion of Switzerland's visits to Lucerne, Rhine Falls, Stein am Rhein and Zurich.

Nestled on the hills, Switzerland is the most beautiful country in the world. Its beauty makes you feel like heaven on earth. This country of Central Europe is also famous for its mountainous terrain with its economic, political and social stability. The natural beauty of the Alps range in the southern region and the associated mountain range in the northwest attracts the whole world.

Switzerland has been a popular shooting destination among Indian filmmakers because of its scenic beauty, captivating and romantic landscapes. Many Indian films have been partially shot here, including Dil Wale Dulhania Le Jayenge, Kuch Kuch Hota Hai, Mohabbatein, Chandni, Chori Chori Chupke Chupke, Darr etc. By the way, there are many such places in Himachal Pradesh, Uttarakhand, Rajasthan, Kashmir, etc. of India, which are not behind Switzerland in terms of natural beauty, beautiful and romantic landscapes. We just need development from the tourism point of view. Switzerland is a rich country. Due to the high income of the citizens, their standard of living is high. Its capital is Bern and the currency is the Swiss franc. It is not a member of the European Union.

Constitution based on the principle of liberty and equality

Switzerland is the Federal Republic. Its constitution is a written document based on the principle of liberty and equality, which outlines the federal political structure of the country and the rights and freedoms of citizens. Here citizens directly participate in the decision-making process at various political levels. This is done through initiatives and referendums, which are proof of direct democracy. According to the constitution, Switzerland is governed by a seven-member Federal Council which leads the government. There is no mention of political parties in the constitution of Switzerland. That is why political parties are not as powerful in the polity as they are in Britain, America and other countries.

Switzerland's Jungfrau: A wonderland of natural beauty

Switzerland has a bicameral system and its legislative powers are also vested in these two houses, the National Council and the Council of States. The government of Switzerland is organized at three levels, i.e., Confederation (national), Canton (state) and commune (municipal). There are 26 cantons in Switzerland. Each canton is autonomous with its own government and parliament. The canton sets policies in areas such as education, health, and policing. Each canton has a number of communes (municipalities) providing roads and other utilities services. The canton and the commune enjoy significant autonomy and make decisions in their own affairs to a large extent. Dual citizenship system is prevalent in Switzerland. According to the Constitution, every canton resident must also be a Swiss citizen. It gives a person the right to both citizenship of the Swiss Federation and citizenship of the canton.

German, French, Italian, and Romansh are the four official languages in Switzerland and people of different cultural groups live here, which underlines the beauty of unity in diversity. Switzerland's judiciary operates at the federal and canton levels. It is the responsibility of the judiciary to ensure that the law is followed.

Christianity is predominant in Switzerland, with the largest number of Roman Catholics and Protestants. Followers of other religions like Islam, Hinduism, Judaism also live here. The Muslim population in Switzerland is about 5%, which is mainly due to immigrants from countries such as Turkey, Bosnia, and Kosovo. Hindus make up about 1% of the population, most of whom are Sri Lankan Tamils. Followers of Judaism are also present in Switzerland, although their population is relatively small.

Ban on wearing burka in public places

It is pertinent to mention here that Switzerland has banned women from wearing hijab, burka or any other form of face covering in public places since January 2025. There is a provision for fines for breaking the law. The ban was imposed as a result of a nationwide referendum held in Switzerland in March 2021. Denmark, Austria, the Netherlands, Bulgaria and other countries have already banned wearing the burqa in public places. Switzerland, like other countries in Europe, has people who do not believe in God or a higher power. These people are non-religious. These people do not have any attachment to established religions.

Education System in Switzerland

Switzerland's education system is divided into several levels. Compulsory education here is 11 years, which is arranged by local municipalities. The medium of instruction is determined by the canton. It can be French, German, Italian or Romansh. 11 years compulsory education is free, including primary school and secondary school. There are also private schools, which is popular for international students. There are many world-class universities and colleges for higher education, offering a variety of degree and diploma programs. Due to being a European business hub, many small business courses are also run at the local level. Thousands of foreign students come here every year for technology, architecture, economics and design courses.

World's Longest Rail Tunnel

Switzerland is also known as the land of tunnels. There are about 1200 tunnels here. The world's longest Gotthard Base Rail Tunnel is in Switzerland. Its length is 57.1 kilometers. Switzerland also has a cog wheel rail service on high hills, which is used to see the natural beauty of the hills or to reach designated destination located on the hill. Cog wheel rails are also called rack railways. It is a special type of railway system for climbing steep slopes. It has an additional "rack rail" in the middle of the track. The train locomotive has one or more geared wheels, which connect with this rack rail, which helps in pulling the train upwards or downwards.

The world's longest rail tunnel in Gotthard, switzerland. Length is 57.1 km.

Famous for manufacturing quality watches

Switzerland is also known for its rich industrial production centers, excellent banking and financial services. There are factories for watch manufacturing, high-quality chocolate, engineering, transportation and other manufacturing industries here.

Switzerland is known for producing high-quality watches and delicious chocolate in the world. It is home to many famous watchmakers such as Rolex, Omega and many famous Swiss chocolate brands of delicious chocolates, "Lindt and Nestle". Cheese production is also an important industry in Switzerland. Swiss cheese is known for its excellent taste and quality. There are many factories in Switzerland in other industries, such as pharmaceuticals, chemicals, and machinery. Switzerland is also a major exporter of high-end watches, chocolates and cheese. The banking and financial services here are excellent. There is black money of corrupt people in Swiss banks. The Swiss bank has the protection of such unethical practices from the Swiss government. The black money of corrupt people from India, Pakistan, Bangladesh etc. is deposited in the bank here.

Since independence, India and Switzerland have enjoyed cordial and friendly relations, based on shared values of democracy and rule of law. India's non-alignment and Switzerland's traditional policy of neutrality have fostered closer understanding between the two countries

Indian Festivals on Foreign Soil

I am fortunate that before concluding the journey, I got an opportunity to participate in the Holi and Jagannath Rath Yatra organized in Prague, the capital of the Czech Republic, with my family. The temperature remains minus 18 degrees here till the first week of March, so the Indian festival of Holi is symbolically celebrated here in June every year, Date: 14th June 2025, Time: 5.30 pm, Pancrase Park Ground. A stage in the grounds, anchors with an instrumentalist on the stage. A crowd of Indian costumed men on the field. Dozens of tents on both sides of the ground, shops decorated in tents, shops with Indian dishes like panipuri, chaat, samosa, jalebi, gulab jamun, rasgula.

A scene from Holi festival in Prague, Czech republic

At some distance to the left and right of the stage, the whole atmosphere was fragrant with the cultural fragrance of India. The festival of colours, Holi, began with the announcement of the anchor. Everyone started celebrating the joy of Rangotsav by showering colors on each other. Some Europeans also joined in, making the atmosphere of the festival enjoyable and attractive. The Holi melody of musical instruments from the stage turned the festival into a dance festival. Foreign tourists also participated in it. It was a very picturesque view. The Indian festival "Holi" was organized by the Bharat Sang Committee. The Indians working here had come in Indian dress with their families. Members of the Indian Embassy were also present on the occasion.

Rath Yatra of Lord Jagannath

On June 29th, 2025, the Rath Yatra was scheduled to be taken out in Prague, the capital of the Czech Republic. It is organized every year by the local unit of ISKCON. It was reported that most people in Luzce, a village in the Czech Republic, have incorporated all the beliefs and traditions of ISKCON into their lives. They regularly recite and studies the verses of Gita every day. Every year, the grand program of Rath Yatra and Krishna Janmashtami is organized by ISKCON in Prague with the help of these people. According to the earlier program, the Rath Yatra formally started from the Old Town Square of Prague at 12 Noon. The presence of thousands of people and the devotional atmosphere created an incomparable wonderfully attractive landscape.

Indian attire. Some natives of the Czech Republic were also involved. The teachings of the Gita on the philosophy of life were being narrated from the stage at the concluding venue of the Rath Yatra with a local Czech translation in English.

Lord Jagannath's Rath Yatra in Prague

Everyone was chanting 'Hare Rama Hare Krishna'. Devotees are thronging the chariot to the tune of devotion and chanting the chants of 'Hare Rama Hare Krishna'. Behind them was a crowd of devotees pulling the chariot. Lord Jagannath, brother Balram and sister Subhadra were riding on the chariot. The journey ended at 3 p.m. in Prague's Old Town. The organisers and most of the devotees were dressed in The cultural programme based on devotion was also based on Hare Rama, Hare Krishna and Gita. There was an arrangement of prasad for everyone. I also got the privilege of participating in the Rath Yatra. Seven seas away, despite the differences in dialect, language, religion, lifestyle, human warmth had tied everyone in the thread of devotional happiness. ISKCON is less than praised for expanding the Sanatani tradition dedicated to humanity on foreign soil. By the way, in many countries like Europe, America etc. the role of ISKCON as the flag bearer of Sanatan for the welfare of humanity and spiritual peace of the individual is commendable.

Europe in the mirror of facts

A brief introduction to Europe is necessary for the completeness of the visit to Czech Republic, Italy, Switzerland, Austria and Germany. From the geographical point of view, there are seven continents on the global map: Europe, Asia, North America, South America, Africa, Australia and Antarctica. Despite differences over the number and boundaries of continents, there is a consensus in the world on seven continents. Europe is the sixth largest continent in size and the third largest continent in population. It is smaller than Asia, Africa, North America and South America, but larger than Australia and Antarctica. Asia is the largest continent in terms of population and size.

Efforts had begun to bring Europe, devastated by the destruction of wars, into the mainstream. The ill effects of the Second World War paved the way for European countries to come together and establish the European Union to achieve prosperity, respect, mutual cooperation and to avoid future wars on the basis of peaceful co-existence. Learning from the destruction of wars, European countries decided to come together and promote economic, political and social cooperation, so that such conflicts could be avoided in future. The formation of the European Union took place in several stages, with the establishment of the European Coal and Steel Community (ECSC) in 1951 being the first stage. The formation of the European Economic Community (EEC) through the Treaty of Rome in 1957 was the second stage and finally the European Union was established in 1993 after the Maastricht Treaty.

European Union – An organization of 27 Countries

The European Union is a political and economic organization of 27 member countries. It regulates economic, social and security policies in the interest of its member countries. The European Union provides a common market and a common currency (Euro) to ensure the free movement of goods, services, capital and people between its member countries in the economic sphere. To ensure a better life for its citizens, the European Union makes laws and policies in the areas of environment, agriculture, transport, energy and consumer protection and also works for the security of the borders of its member countries, combating terrorism, protecting human rights, improving social security, education and health services. In short, it can be said that the European Union conducts various activities to promote peace, socio-cultural cooperation, prosperity and security among its member countries.

Currently 27 countries - Austria, Belgium, Bulgaria, Croatia, Cyprus, Czech Republic, Denmark, Estonia, Finland, France, Germany, Greece, Hungary, Ireland, Italy, Latvia, Lithuania, Luxembourg, Malta, Netherlands, Poland, Portugal, Romania, Slovakia, Slovenia, Spain and Sweden are members of the European Union. Luxembourg is the richest country in the European Union in terms of per capita income, and its citizens enjoy high incomes. It is a major center for large private banking. Its financial sector is the largest contributor to its economy, but Hungary, once prosperous, is currently the poorest country in the European Union. The most expensive country in Europe is Switzerland. The cost of living in Switzerland is much higher than the EU average. Many other European countries also have high living costs. Iceland, Luxembourg, Denmark and Ireland are prominent among them, but Switzerland is at the top. Bulgaria is the cheapest country in Europe. This country is a popular choice for budget travelers due to the low cost of accommodation, food and transportation. Burqa ban is in force in many countries of Europe. Wearing burqa in public places is banned in countries like France, Belgium, Denmark, Austria, Netherlands, Bulgaria, and Switzerland. In addition, partial bans are in force in some states of Germany. The United Kingdom separated itself from the European Union. Therefore, it is no longer a part of the European Union.

The European Union received the Nobel Peace Prize in 2012

The European Union received the Nobel Peace Prize in 2012 for its invaluable contribution in promoting peace, reconciliation, democratic values and human rights in Europe since its inception. However, every year the Nobel Peace Prize is given by the five-member Nobel Committee appointed by the Norwegian Parliament (Starting) as per the will of Alfred Nobel. The Nobel Peace Prize ceremony is held every year in Oslo,Norway, while other Nobel Prizes are given in Stockholm, Sweden.

Eurozone's important role in economic dynamism

The economy of the European Union is strong and developed. The role of the Eurozone is important in maintaining the dynamism of its economic development. The Eurozone comprises those countries of the European Union which have accepted the Euro as their national currency. At present, 20 countries of the European Union are members of the Eurozone. To join the Eurozone, member countries have to control their inflation rate and keep government debt, fiscal deficit and interest rates at a certain level. The main objective of the Eurozone is to promote economic integration among the member countries of the European Union. The use of the Euro promotes trade and investment. It also helps member countries to deal with economic shocks. The 20 member countries in the Eurozone include Austria, Belgium, Croatia, Cyprus, Estonia, Finland, France, Germany, Greece, Ireland, Italy, Latvia, Lithuania, Luxembourg, Malta, Netherlands, Portugal, Slovakia, Slovenia and Spain.

29 European countries in Schengen

According to the United Nations, there are 44 countries in the continent of Europe. All countries are independent and sovereign. Permission of that country is required for entry into any sovereign country for tourism, business, education or employment. Visa is an official document issued by the government, which allows entry, stay or travel in that country. There are many types of visas, such as tourist visa, student visa, business visa etc., which are issued as per the requirement for various purposes. Schengen visa is important for travelling to Europe. This visa includes travel to 29 European countries of the Schengen area. There is no passport control at the borders between these countries. If you have a valid visa or residence permit of any one of these countries, you can travel to other Schengen area countries.

For the first time in 1985, the circulation of Schengen visa started based on an agreement reached in Schengen, Luxembourg between five European countries - Belgium, France, Germany, Luxembourg and Netherlands. Its objective was to eliminate internal borders between European countries and promote the free movement of people, goods and services. This agreement came into force in 1995 and has been expanding since then. The Schengen area currently includes 29 countries, including most of the member countries of the European Union and some non-EU countries. To obtain a Schengen visa, an application has to be submitted to the embassy or consulate of the concerned country along with passport, travel itinerary, proof of residence, application fee, financial statement, travel insurance etc. But Indian passport holders have to submit their visa application at application centers like VFS Global.

It has many centers in India. After preliminary scrutiny of the applicant's biometric data (fingerprints and photos) and application, the visa application is sent to the concerned embassy / consulate in India. Within about 15 days, the visa is approved and the applicant receives it by post at his address. Schengen visa is a document in the form of a sticker which is pasted on the passport of the traveler. Under the Schengen visa, one is allowed to travel freely to the 29 countries of the Schengen area for the duration of the visa. Under a single-entry visa, one is allowed to enter the Schengen area once, while under a multiple-entry visa, one is allowed to travel more than once during the visa period. To travel to countries other than the 29 European countries of the Schengen area, a visa has to be obtained from the embassy of the concerned country. To travel to the Schengen area, visa holders are required to carry a valid passport and travel insurance with them.

Bible is the holy book of Christianity

The number of Christians in Europe is the highest. Christianity is one of the major religions of the world. The Bible is considered to be the holy book in Christianity. In Christianity, God is considered to be a trinity, which includes God the Father, the Son (Jesus Christ) and the Holy Spirit. That is, in Christianity, God is three elements and they understand God in three forms: God the Father, his son Jesus Christ (Jesus Christ) and the Holy Spirit. Most Christian sects consider Jesus Christ to be the son of God and the Holy Trinity to be the second person. The Holy Spirit is considered to be the power and presence of God. In Christianity, prayers are offered to God with love, reverence and faith.

The position of the church was very important in medieval Europe. Religious activities were conducted from here. It was not only a religious institution, but also a political, social and cultural power. The church influenced almost every aspect of people's lives, including education, justice, art and politics.

Christianity was founded in the first century. The faith and tradition of Christianity is based on the personality and teachings of Jesus Christ. All the commandments mentioned in the Bible are at the center of Christianity. Christians believe that Jesus Christ is the son of God and his sacrifice was for the salvation of mankind. Scholars have considered Christianity to be a monotheistic religion at the center of faith and tradition and have rejected polytheistic culture and atheism. There is no trace of religious fanaticism among Christians. In the Christian community, emphasis is laid on building relationships based on love and brotherhood and serving each other. The church plays an important role in Christianity, where Christians gather to pray, worship and live together in the community. In Christianity, Christmas is celebrated on December 25 to commemorate the birthday of Jesus Christ. Europe has the highest number of Christians. These include various sects such as Catholics, Protestants and Orthodox, who follow their own beliefs and practices.

Non-Christians are also present in Europe. Followers of Islam, Judaism, Buddhism, Hinduism and other East Asian religions are also present in Europe. However, their number is much less than that of Christians.

Islam is a monotheistic religion

Bosnia, Herzegovina, Albania, Kosovo, North Macedonia and some Russia parts of the Balkan region have a good population of Muslims, who belongs to Islam. Islam was founded in the sixth century. Islam is a monotheistic religion and Allah is considered the God of this religion. Mohammed is the prophet of Allah. There are five basic duties prescribed for the followers of Islam, which are also known as the five pillars of Islam: Shahadat (declaration of faith), Salat (prayer), Zakat (charity), Sawm (fasting) and Haj (pilgrimage). In Islam, only Allah is considered worthy of worship. Quran is the holy book of Muslims. Quran started being revealed in Arabic language to Hazrat Mohammad for the guidance of humans. Holy Quran is divided into many parts. Mosque plays an important role in conducting religious activities. Jewish community has been present in Europe since ancient times. Due to Jewish genocide during the Second World War, this number has reduced a lot.

The presence of Hindus in Europe cannot be denied. Along with this, millions of Indian families working in multinational companies and engaged in business are living in Europe and contributing to the strengthening of the economy there. In such a situation, it becomes necessary to discuss the religion of Indian origin. Sanatan Dharma is a prominent religion of the Indian subcontinent, which means eternal or 'everlasting' i.e. which has no beginning and no end. Sanatan Dharma, also known as Hinduism, is the oldest religion in the world. It has been developing for thousands of years and is still alive today, which proves its continuity and antiquity.

Sanatan Dharma, the key to human welfare

Sanatan Dharma is the key to the welfare of all human beings based on Vedic scriptures. It is a means of mental peace and spiritual progress. Considering the earth as a family (Vasudhaiva Kutumbakam - वसधैवु कुटुम्बकम) , the resolution of happiness and welfare of humanity (Sarvajan SukhayeSarvajan Hitaye) is at the center of this religion. Apart from Vedic scriptures, Gita and Ramayana are such works, by following which the welfare of all human beings is possible. Ramayana teaches the art of living life peacefully, while Gita provides detailed knowledge of life philosophy and rituals and makes one experience the divine power in every particle.

It considers every living being as a part of God. Sanatan Dharma is also monotheistic, but its external form is polytheistic. It mentions the incarnation of God in various forms many times for the protection of religion. Sanatan Dharma is called polytheistic due to the worship of different forms of the same God. By the way, it is clearly stated in the Rigveda that "Ekam Sad Vipra Bahudha Vadanti" i.e. the same God is called by many names by the wise people. In the Sanatan tradition, religion is also called the medicine of humanity.

Religious freedom is respected in most European countries. All people have the freedom to follow religious practices based on their faith and belief. Despite this, the inclination of people towards religion is gradually decreasing here. Especially in Western Europe, the number of non-religious people is continuously increasing, but it has no effect on the followers of Islam. Non-religious people mean those who have not associated themselves with the beliefs and traditions of any religion.

Russia-Ukraine War: A Glimpse

It is necessary to discuss Ukraine, which has been sacrificing itself in the fire of war for more than three and a half years. Ukraine is a country located in Eastern Europe, but earlier it was a republic of the Soviet Union. Ukraine came into existence after the dissolution of the Soviet Union on 26 December 1991. However, relations between the two countries have been tense since the Russian occupation of Crimea in 2014.

Russia's objective was to prevent Ukraine from joining NATO outside its sphere of influence. This is also the declared reason for the war. 30 of NATO's 32 member countries are from Europe. NATO is also known as the North Atlantic Treaty Organization. The NATO headquarters is the political and administrative center of the alliance. It is located in Brussels, Belgium. It is a military and political alliance. This alliance works on the principle of collective defense, which means that an attack on one member will be considered an attack on all members. This is also the basic principle of NATO mentioned in Article-5 of the Atlantic Treaty.

Russia has been considering Ukraine's desire to join NATO, the military alliance of Western countries, as a security threat to itself. Russia wanted Ukraine to remain a neutral country. Russia did not want Ukraine to form close ties with Western countries or strengthen its sovereignty. Russian President Putin believes that Western countries have continuously expanded NATO since the dissolution of the Soviet Union, which is a threat to Russia from a strategic point of view.

There has been a lot of loss of life and property in this war. Ukraine has suffered more losses than Russia. More than 20 percent of the Ukrainian territory has been occupied by Russia. A large number of Ukrainian citizens have been forced to take refuge in European countries. Ukraine has been devastated a lot. Apart from military aid and moral support, NATO has not yet gathered the courage to grant membership to Ukraine. In such a situation, Ukraine should take a decision based on ground reality. There is a saying in the rural areas of India that it is better to lose the yard than to lose the station.

The world wants peace. In this episode, Indian Prime Minister Narendra Modi had made a positive effort for a peaceful settlement. He also visited Russia and Ukraine. He told the Russian President that this is not the time for war, but due to Zelensky's immaturity and the negative thinking of some European leaders, the attempt to reach a peace agreement between the two countries failed. India has adopted neutral diplomacy in the whole matter. Currently, US President Donald Trump is trying for a peace agreement. In this sequence, he has already had one meeting with his Russian counterpart in Alaska and the second meeting with Ukrainian President Zelensky and European leaders at the White House. But the war is being prolonged due to Zelensky's stubbornness beyond the ground realities and the short sightedness of some European leaders. Ukraine will have to bear the burnt because of this.

Road traffic is also an important part of transport in Europe. Transportation of goods and passengers is included in this. Policies for road transport in the European Union are in place with the aim of promoting efficient, safe, secure and environmentally friendly mobility. Road is an important means of freight and passenger transport. Road transport has been linked with rail, sea and inland waterways.

Important role of Waze app in smooth road traffic

There is a waze app to make road traffic easy and smooth in Europe, due to which guidance of the direction of the destination, speed prescribed for transport on the highway, speed of the vehicle, lane related information, vehicle parked ahead on the road and information related to construction work comes on this screen with alert. The alarm also automatically indicates if the speed of the vehicle increases beyond the prescribed limit. Maximum speed is prescribed everywhere for transport on the highway. Only in Germany there is no maximum speed limit for transport on the highway and the highway here is toll free. In many countries of Europe, glass freeway sound barriers have been built on the highway to protect the population from noise pollution.

There are many rules and laws in the European Union to regulate road transport and prevent accidents, which include working hours, driving time, rest periods and fees for professional road transport etc. Road transport is a major source of carbon emissions. To reduce emissions and make road transport more sustainable in Europe, attention is being paid to alternative fuels and energy efficiency.

Signal light for pedestrians

The traffic system of tourist places and major cities of Europe is smooth and organized. Traffic signaling is of high quality. Police is not seen at any traffic post, yet the traffic remains organized and controlled. A separate signal lamp is installed on the zebra crossing for pedestrians. Pedestrians cross the road only when the light of the lamp is green, but where there is no signal lamp on the zebra crossing, pedestrians cross the road without hesitation and the responsibility of establishing coordination lies with the driver. Bus, metro, tram or bus and tram service is operated under public transport in all major cities. The entire traffic system is computerized, due to which the passenger gets information about the timetable and stoppage of the transport on mobile. The option of buying travel tickets of public transport is also available on mobile. Computerized display boards are installed at all stoppages, on which information related to the arrival and departure of vehicles is displayed. Apart from this, online booking service of many private agencies is available for taxis. During the entire journey, the sound of horn was not heard even in the event of traffic jam. Following traffic rules is a part of the behaviour of people here.

Trains run on hydrogen gas in Germany

The train service in Europe is a wide and modern network, which allows passengers to travel between different cities and countries. High-speed trains make it possible to travel between several cities in a few hours. Regional trains are a good arrangement for travelling to small cities and villages, while sleeper trains are a comfortable option for long distance travel. During the journey to Florence, Pisa, Venice and Verona, I got the opportunity to see and understand the train service closely. All the main stations are connected to the market complex. There is an underpass for changing platforms. There is no overbridge anywhere. Information about the arrival and departure of trains and platforms is displayed on the display board. All the bogies of the train are air-conditioned. There is a computerized display board outside and inside each bogie. The train number and route are displayed on the display board outside the bogie, while the display board inside the bogie displays the information about the temperature of the bogie, speed of the train, next station and the picture of the passengers sitting in the bogie. Since the bogies are interconnected, one can go to any bogie inside the train. In terms of fare and convenience, bogies are divided into three categories, standard, premium and business. The maximum speed of a regional train is 160 kilometers per hour, while the maximum speed of a highspeed train is 260 kilometers per hour. Germany's train service is more advanced than Italy. Train operations in Germany have started on hydrogen gas. France is also not behind in this era, while a project to start hydrogen-powered trains is under process in Italy. The world's longest rail tunnel is located in Gotthard, Switzerland. Its length is 57.1 kilometers.

Compensation to air passengers

Airplanes are very convenient for long distance travel in Europe. Europe has many major airports like Heathrow, Paris Charles de Gaulle, Amsterdam Schiphol, Frankfurt, Madrid, Istanbul etc., which connect different cities and countries. These airports are good centers for traveling both within and outside Europe. There is a provision for the airline company to pay 600 euros (60,000 rupees) as compensation to the passenger if the flight is delayed for more than three hours, except in natural disasters and special circumstances. Probably this is also a reason for timely flight operations. The European Union ensures that aviation safety remains at a high level.

Climate change is a challenge for human civilization

Climate change is one of a challenge for human civilization. Carbon emissions are the main reason for this. Human activities are at the root of the changes in weather patterns on the global stage like increase in temperature and natural disasters. This includes burning of fossil fuels (coal, oil, gas) and deforestation. Greenhouse gases like carbon dioxide and methane are factors in temperature rise. Apart from this, there are also natural causes like volcanic activity and changes in the energy of the sun.

The role of the United Nations is important in curbing carbon emissions. The United Nations provides a platform for global climate negotiations, in which historic decisions like the Kyoto Protocol and the Paris Agreement have been taken and this has encouraged international cooperation and action to tackle climate change.

The United Nations brings together all countries and stakeholders to deal with complex climate issues and promote global climate action and publishes scientific reports and information through organizations like the Intergovernmental Panel on Climate Change (IPCC), which are important for policy makers.

The European continent remains active in curbing carbon emissions. The European Union has set a goal of becoming a climate-neutral economy by 2050 under the European Green Deal, which includes a legally binding target of reducing greenhouse gas emissions by at least 55% compared to 1990 levels by 2030. India is also not behind in curbing carbon emissions. It has set a goal of reducing its carbon intensity by 45% compared to 2005 levels by 2030 and achieving net-zero by 2070. This also includes expansion of renewable energy and afforestation. India is increasing green energy production capacity from non-fossil sources such as sunlight, wind, water.

Green energy is a clean and environmentally friendly energy that is obtained from renewable sources and has no harmful effect on the natural environment. It reduces dependence on fossil fuels (coal, gas and oil) and reduces the emission of harmful greenhouse gases that contribute to global warming. Solar energy (generating electricity using sunlight), wind energy (generating electricity from wind turbines using wind) and hydroelectricity (generating electricity from

the flow of water) are the main sources of green energy. Not all renewable energy is green, while most green energy is renewable. Burning organic substances such as wood produces biomass energy, which is renewable, but it releases greenhouse gases, so it is not considered green energy.

Cycling, walking, rolling and using public transport instead of driving can help in reducing carbon emissions. In the field of green energy, work is constantly being done on green hydrogen, which aims to develop hydrogen fuel technology. Hydrogen is a clean fuel option. When the fuel cell ends, it produces only water, which is a better option than CNG in terms of pollution. A hydrogen-powered car has two tanks, highly compressed and low compressed. Strong tanks and pipes are used due to the flammability of hydrogen gas. Under this technology, oxygen is passed through the chamber from one side and hydrogen from the other. The energy released from this chemical reaction runs the vehicle. Water comes out instead of smoke, hence there is no pollution. Germany is currently ahead in green hydrogen production technology.

The world's longest sea tunnel

The 'Channel Tunnel' is the world's longest sea tunnel, also known as Eurotunnel or "Chunnel". It is a 50.5 km long railway tunnel. 37.9 km of it is built in the sea. This tunnel connects England (United Kingdom) to France. The Channel Tunnel is actually made up of three parallel tunnels: two main rail tunnels (one from Britain to France and the other from France to Britain) and a smaller service tunnel. The rail tunnels are used for passenger and freight trains, while the service tunnel is used for ventilation and access. It provides a vital route for travel and trade between Europe and Britain. This tunnel is the result of a massive engineering project.

This tunnel is operated by Getlink, which also operates Le Shuttle service for vehicles (cars, vans etc.) and passengers. Eurostar is a high-speed train service, which passes through the tunnel. It provides a fast and pleasant journey between the United Kingdom and France. The Channel Tunnel is a vital link between the United Kingdom and mainland Europe, facilitating the transport of both passengers and goods. It is a unique infrastructure that facilitates year-round travel under the English Channel.

Social security is the priority of the European Union

The European Union emphasizes on social security, worklife balance and social inclusion. Here there is universal health care, free education, strong labor protection laws and liberal welfare programs in areas such as unemployment insurance, retirement pension and public housing. The family has an important place here, but the joint family system is heading towards its end. In the Czech Republic, it is on its end. Europe has a mixture of different ethnic groups, languages and cultures, which makes it a culturally rich continent.

In Europe, criminal cases like theft, snatching, pickpocketing etc. are negligible. The people here are kind and well behaved. Despite the differences in country, language and culture, the feeling of kindness towards tourists is a symbol of their cultural heritage of humanity.